"When Alba Huerta promises you a 'Southern' cocktail, she delivers an undeniably delicious, inventive drink that's inspired by a deep, passionate study of our region. This book traces the steps of her creative process with thoroughly researched history lessons, clear-eyed observations of her own experience, and an undeniable sense of Southern hospitality—all expressed through cocktails that will have you raising your glass for more."

• ASHLEY CHRISTENSEN •
chef/owner of Poole's Diner and author of *Poole's*

—————•—————

"Alba has re-created the classic Southern libations with ingenuity and purpose: The ingenuity is her gracious and insightful tour of the culinary heritage of the rural South and the saltwater cities through her culinary craft cocktails; the purpose is deliciousness."

• DALE DEGROFF •
author of *The Craft of the Cocktail*

Julep

Alba Huerta
& Marah Stets

Julep

SOUTHERN
COCKTAILS
REFASHIONED

Photography by
Julie Soefer

LORENA JONES BOOKS
An imprint of TEN SPEED PRESS
California | New York

To my parents, who've loved me with all
their souls and raised me to be strong

Contents

Acknowledgments

I was managing Anvil the first time that Kenneth Freeman walked into the bar and asked me for a job. I sent him away because he didn't have a resume in hand. The following day, he returned with the precise thing I'd asked of him, but his shirt was quite wrinkled. "Son, you can't be runnin' around town at 4 o'clock in the afternoon asking people for a job and looking like the cat chewed your shirt," I remember teasing. So I turned him away again and sure enough he came right back—wearing a shirt so heavily starched it could stand on its own and a resume so thorough it left no question unanswered. I'm still not sure how he pulled it together so fast, but all I needed to know was that he could. It was many years later that he became the opening general manager of Julep but I knew long before that, from many years of working with him, that Kenny would always deliver what was asked of him. His leadership, creativity, and strength helped mold our staff into fine and talented individuals and without him, moments in my career would not be as memorable. We nicknamed him The Yeti, and to this day, he's out there in the world steadily kicking ass.

It also goes without saying that without the day-to-day work and dedication of Julep's bar staff, present and past, this book would not have been possible. I consider myself lucky to see the staff grow and be a part of their transformative process, as they are also a part of mine. Going from being a bartender to a bar owner was a huge leap and they stayed with me all the way. Many of the recipes in this book and at Julep are developed by committee and I am so grateful for everyone on the team who've made these creations possible.

The photography in this book can all be credited to my Taurus sister, Julie Soefer. Before we opened the bar, I invited her to come to Kentucky to buy a barrel of bourbon. She's been on Team Julep since day one and when the opportunity to do a book came, she was the only photographer on my list. She had photographed all of our press releases, all of our menus, and now this beautiful book. She, Claudia Casbarian, and Amanda Medsger worked tirelessly styling and perfecting every image. Thank you, ladies, for your hard work and professionalism.

Also a big thank you goes to Pam Kuhl-Linscomb and Dan Linscomb and Colby Goetschius of Kuhl-Linscomb who generously let us borrow textures, glassware, spoons, and all of the finery for the photo shoot. Their kindness is what Houston is all about, and I can't wait to put this book in their hands.

To those closest to me—Scott, Aracely, and Checo—thank you for being my support system in life, though the many edits and long nights, and for your love and understanding. And to all of the strong women in my life, especially my grandmother, who taught herself to read and write at the age of sixty-five. Thank you for showing me that there are always new possibilities and always work well worth doing.

Thanks from the bottom of my heart to Marah Stets, my brilliant writer who wins the prize (that no one wants) of having universal patience and being the world-class wrangler of me. I will miss our time together and am proud of what we've created. She brings out the best in everyone and has brought so much joy to my life.

Deep gratitude and admiration go to the Southern Foodways Alliance. It's my pleasure to serve on this organization's board and be a part of the ever-changing American South. It was at the SFA Women at Work Symposium that I met Lorena Jones, my publisher, and David Black, my agent—a killer combination of talent and grace. They conceptualized this book even before we put pen to paper. Thank you both for believing in the project and bringing it to fruition. Thanks, too, to Ten Speed Press designer Betsy Stromberg, production manager Jane Chinn, publicity director Kristin Casemore, associate marketing director Allison Renzulli, and their many colleagues, who have supported this book.

John T. Edge, the Director of the SFA, and I met at Blacksmith Coffee Shop in Houston two years before I opened Julep. I can honestly say that meeting a person with such true devotion to his family, friends, work, and purpose has helped form who I am today. Thank you, John T. (don't forget the T.), for being a

great example of how to live a meaningful life. Through the SFA, I found a family that is brilliant, progressive, and embracing of all cultures, food, and people. I've made friends for a lifetime. The theme for SFA's intensive three-day symposium in 2017 is "El Sur Latino" and this Mexican-American couldn't be more proud and excited. Thank you for being a part of our creative process, menus, and this book.

It would only make sense that the SFA's philosophy would resonate with me because it encapsulates the same values as the city I grew up in. Although it is not my birth city, Houston, Texas, has been my home for almost my entire life. Julep was born here and the details of the program are influenced by the dynamics that envelop Houston. As an immigrant, I was fortunate to be raised in a forward-thinking society that is rich with diverse cultures and opportunities to grow and advance. My family was one of the many who were granted amnesty through the 1986 Immigration Reform and Control Act, and it was life-changing. As my family and I became citizens of America, this beautiful city always made us feel welcome, included, empowered, and loved. Thank you, Houston, for welcoming me, my family, and Julep with open arms.

Two major advocates of my work have always been my parents, Sergio and Maria Alba. My dad, who was eight when his father died, making him the de facto head of the household, and my mother, who escaped from a convent in order to make a life of her own, have shown me how to achieve the impossible, be resilient, love one another for almost fifty years, and always work harder than the day before. I've been graced that they are just twenty years older than me. We've grown together, learned a new language together, and they've loved me unconditionally—even when my career choice interfered with family gatherings. My spirit is their spirit.

Introduction

When I started work on this book, I knew I wanted the recipes to be more than unique and storytelling. I also wanted them to be makeable at home because it's only so much fun to read about delicious drinks—mixing them for yourself and others is what makes these drinks truly enjoyable. With that in mind, there are a few tools, techniques, terms, and ingredients you need to be comfortable with to make these refashioned Southern cocktails.

Tools

You don't need a huge arsenal of fancy gadgets to make a great cocktail, but a few well-made tools are essential.

Cocktail shaker • I prefer the Koriko brand shaker. It consists of one small, weighted cup and a larger weighted cup that fit together to form a tight seal so you can vigorously shake a cocktail. The cups are sold individually or as sets of two (one large and one smaller cup); I recommend that you buy the latter.

Mixing glass • For mixing stirred drinks, we use a 500-milliliter heavy-duty mixing glass made by Yarai. This specific size and brand works perfectly with the barspoon and strainers I recommend. It's okay to use a different size or brand but be aware that the glass's mouth may be too large or small for the strainers I suggest to effectively hold back the ice.

Muddler • This tool is used to press ingredients such as herbs or fruits to release their oils, aromas, and juices. We use a natural, untreated wood muddler.

Jigger • This two-sided measuring tool comes in a variety of sizes. The best choice is a Japanese-style jigger with a 1- to 2-ounce capacity on one side and a ½- to ¾-ounce capacity on the other side. There are graduated lines inside each cup to measure smaller increments.

Barspoon • Used for stirring and some-times measuring, a standard barspoon has a capacity of 1 teaspoon (5 milliliters/0.17 ounce). A few cocktails in this book use the barspoon as a measurement. This is because well-balanced drinks require precision, which sometimes means meas-uring by the barspoon, not the ounce. With a 500-milliliter mixing glass, use a 30-centimeter-long barspoon.

Strainers • We use three types of strainers:

A HAWTHORNE STRAINER is used for cocktails shaken in the Koriko shaker. It has a coil that fits tightly inside the rim of the glass so that it holds back all of the ice and any herbs, citrus, other large ingredients from the shaken drink.

A JULEP STRAINER has a bowl-shaped perforated head that fits snugly over the mixing glass. It was originally used for drinking juleps to hold back the crushed ice when the drinker took a sip. We use it for stirred drinks that are served up.

A FINE STRAINER has a fine-mesh straining bowl. We fine-strain shaken drinks served up and some drinks that include herbs and fruit. (See page 6 for technique notes on this.)

Dropper • A glass eyedropper is useful for measuring small amounts of ingredients, such as tinctures and vanilla. I like 2-ounce glass bottles to store these kinds of ingre-dients in the bar. Glass is best because it does not absorb flavors.

Citrus press • A hinged press is the best tool for juicing citrus because it thoroughly extracts the fruit's juice while holding back most of the pulp.

Juicer • A few cocktails require juicing of ingredients other than citrus. A centrifugal juicer does the best job.

Soda siphon and CO_2 cartridges • This tool is great for carbonating filtered water and verjus (see page 111). I recommend iSi brand siphons because they vigilantly test their products; read the assembly and usage instructions very carefully.

Cocktail picks • Picks made from bamboo are a good choice. I recommend 4- to 4¼-inch size.

Glassware

The glass chosen is elemental to the style of the drink. In many cases, in fact, the glass used is part of the definition of the cocktail. For example, a Collins glass is used for a Collins and a julep cup is used for a julep. It is important to use the glass size called for in a recipe. When we call for a small or large coupe, it's because of the volume of the cocktail. Using a larger coupe than is called for will make the cocktail look like a tiny pool of liquid at the bottom of a large bowl; and if you use a smaller coupe than is called for you risk the drink overflowing!

Techniques

A few techniques are important to ensure your cocktails have the best flavor, the proper texture, and are served at the correct temperature.

Muddling and pressing • Use a muddler for both of these methods. Muddling is used to completely pulverize an ingredient, such as a fruit or vegetable. Pressing is gentler and is usually done to herbs to release their oils. The difference is important. When pressing the mint for the Mint Julep (page 17), for example, if you were to thoroughly muddle the mint, you'd release its bitter elements. For the fig in the Vinegar & Rye (page 105), on the other hand, you do need to thoroughly pulverize it because shaking alone won't fully incorporate the fruit into the cocktail.

Shaking • Correctly shaking a cocktail is important to chill it as well as to ensure that an appropriate amount of dilution occurs as the ice melts slightly. In the Ramos Gin Fizz (page 158) I describe the proper technique for shaking a cocktail so that the drink is perfectly shaken and your arms do not become too tired. (No other cocktail in this book requires such a long shake.) When a formula says to "dry shake" the mixture, it means to shake the ingredients without ice. We use this technique to ensure that cocktails made with eggs are partially emulsified before adding the ice.

Fine-straining • To fine-strain a shaken cocktail, attach the Hawthorne strainer to the shaker and hold a fine strainer in your other hand. Pour the cocktail through both strainers simultaneously.

Chilling glasses • Drinks that are served up are best in chilled glasses to help keep them cold. Glasses can be chilled in the freezer, but be careful that there are not aromatic items in there that might impart other flavors to the glasses. Alternatively, fill glasses with cracked ice and soda water and let stand for a few minutes. Drain thoroughly before pouring in the cocktail.

Ice • Ice is much more than just a way of chilling a cocktail. Because it is part of the dilution process, I consider it to be as much an ingredient as any other part of the cocktail. This is why we have a Kold-Draft ice machine at Julep. It makes very dense ice using filtered water. In addition, it freezes the cubes slowly so that they are clear. Because the ice is so dense, its rate of dilution is much slower than regular ice, which means a cocktail will maintain its balance and strength over a longer period of time. Knowing you won't have this tool at home, the cocktails in this book call for three different types of ice:

1¼-INCH CUBES are the most utilized ice. We use cubes this size for shaking and stirring cocktails. We serve just about everything with this size ice, from water to highballs to the pour of bourbon ordered "with just one ice cube." (A 1-inch cube would be also be fine if that's what you have.)

2-INCH CUBES are used in certain bitter and boozy cocktails, such as the Old-Fashioned (page 146) and Truth & Slant (page 106), in which we want to slow the rate of dilution even more. In these cases, it's important to preserve the cold temperature because it is an elemental part of the structure.

CRUSHED ICE is used for cocktails that are composed of juices and sweeteners that need to be diluted faster. Crushing ice into smaller pieces ensures that it will melt more quickly. Practical methods for crushing ice at home are to lightly crush it in a blender; use a Lewis bag and mallet (easily found online; see page 205); or buy a crushed ice maker.

Alcohol Proof

The proof of an alcoholic product is an indication of how much ethanol, or alcohol, is in it. It is expressed as a number, which is double the percentage of alcohol by volume (ABV) contained in the product. In other words, an 80-proof bourbon contains 40 percent alcohol by volume. A couple of other distinctions are important: A spirit that has a true "bonded" designation is 100 proof and an "overproof" spirit is more than 100 proof.

Many recipes in this book indicate a specific proof of bourbon or rye. These are chosen carefully and are determined by the cocktail's structure and the rate of dilution, which is dictated in part by the amount and format of the ice. Every cocktail is special, and the alcohol content of a spirit is as important as the other ingredients.

Bitters

Bitters fall into one of two categories: Non-potable bitters, like the ones described here and used throughout this book, are used by the drop to season drinks. Potable bitters are used in a larger quantity and sometimes as blending spirits in cocktails. These include Italian amari, such as Campari, and bitter digestifs, such as Underberg.

Many of my cocktail recipes call for a type and brand of bitters, and these are not interchangeable. The cocktail's formula depends on the specific type called for. One or two drops can really dramatically change the entire drink. Following are some of the types and brands of bitters I use most often, at the bar and in this book. Try to avoid glycerin-based bitters because they often taste synthetic.

Abbott's • Along with Peychaud's and Angostura, this is one of the most famous cocktail bitters, and it is the most successful style of bitters that uses Angostura bark as the signature flavor ingredient. Abbott's is aged for several months in wood before being bottled.

Angostura • Perhaps the most utilized bitters, this was first produced in the city of Angostura. It does not contain Angostura bark. It is a key ingredient in many classic cocktails, such as the old-fashioned, Champagne cocktail, and the Manhattan. It is also utilized as an aromatic and sprinkled or misted over the foam of drinks.

Bittermens Orange Citrate • This isn't actually a bitters, but it is made by a bitters company. Riffing on the flavors of a classic orange cream soda syrup, they created a concentrated orange cream tincture and modified it with a heavy dose of citric acid. The result is sweet, sour, tart, and creamy but not bitter at all.

Chocolate (Scrappy's) • Organic toasted cacao nibs bring this blend to life. With just a hint of spice and oak, this bitters imparts the essence of chocolate flavor without sweetness.

Orange (Regan's) • Created by Gary Regan, the label includes "No. 6" because he perfected the recipe on his sixth attempt. It is produced by The Sazerac Company of New Orleans. I particularly like that it's dry with cardamom and caraway notes. It's a key ingredient of a truly classic Martini.

Peychaud's • This famous bitters was originally created circa 1830 by Antoine Amédée Peychaud, a Creole apothecary who settled in New Orleans, Louisiana, in 1795. It is a gentian-based bitters, comparable to Angostura bitters but with a lighter body, sweeter taste, and more floral aroma. Peychaud's Bitters is the definitive component of the Sazerac cocktail.

Smoked Chili (Hella) • This small-batch company uses smoked pasilla de Oaxaca chiles as the main flavoring in this bitters. It adds a spicy component and depth to a cocktail.

Aromatized Wines and Vermouth

I use a variety of aromatized wines and vermouths in my cocktails. As with bitters, these are not really interchangeable because each has singular characteristics that play a role in a cocktail. Following are the types I use often at the bar and in the cocktails in this book.

Byrrh • An aromatized wine-based aperitif made of red wine, mistelle, and quinine, with a deep red color and a pronounced dry bitterness balanced with rich, red fruit.

Carpano Antica • The first recipe for this vermouth was recorded by Guiseppe Carpano in 1786. It is a complex vermouth that is deep red in color and has a flavor that is ripe with fig, cherries, chocolate, candied orange, vanilla, warm baking spices, and "garrigue" herbs, meaning fragrant varieties, such as thyme, rosemary, and juniper.

Carpano Bianco • An Italian off-dry, white vermouth. Ginger and flowers are the dominant aromas with a lightly bitter herbaciousness on the palate.

Cocchi Americano Rosa • This rose-colored aperitif is based on a Brachetto d'Acqui wine, and it has the floral and rich berry notes typical of the famous sparkling wine of the same variety. Its flavor is rounded out with notes of ginger and bitters.

Cocchi Torino • For its 120th anniversary in 2011, Italian producer Giulio Cocchi resumed production of its original recipe for Vermouth di Torino, first offered in 1891. It is based on estate-grown Moscato wine and includes vibrant, spicy botanicals, such as cocoa, citrus, and rhubarb. Vermouth di Torino is one of only two protected geographical designations for vermouth (the other one is the Dolin Dry).

Dolin Blanc • The clear, sweet Blanc variety of vermouth was first created and made famous by Dolin in Chambéry long before Italian producers replicated the style as bianco. This product brings minerality and brightness to cocktails.

Dolin Dry • This vermouth is distinguished by its dry, fresh, and clean profile, which comes from a delicate wine base and more than thirty Alpine herbs. It has a fresh and elegant nose and a subtle and complex palate. In the 1930s, Chambéry earned France's only protected designation of origin for vermouth.

Miró Rojo • This well-rounded, wormwood-forward sweet red vermouth has lovely dry, herbaceous qualities.

Suze • This is the quintessential French gentian-based aperitif. It is saffron gold in color, with sweet, lightly floral, and citrusy undertones that support the muscular earthy bitterness of the foraged gentian root.

Citrus Juices

I use only freshly squeezed citrus juices in cocktails because their flavor is brightest within the few hours just after they're pressed. The best tool for juicing citrus at home is a hinged press (see page 2). I recommend straining fresh juice through a fine strainer (see page 2). In general, a lime or lemon will give you about 1 ounce strained juice, an orange will give you about 2 ounces of strained juice, and a grapefruit gives you about 4½ ounces of strained juice. Use fresh juice within 6 hours.

Garnishes

I think the garnish is just as important as the other components of a cocktail. The herbs, fruit, and other ingredients that adorn a drink contribute visual appeal, aroma, and flavor, so use the freshest possible ingredients for this final flourish. Following are notes regarding some specific garnishes.

Citrus zest • Use a sharp vegetable peeler (or zester) to remove the zest, being careful not to remove any of the bitter pith. When garnishing with citrus zest, hold it with the outer skin directly over the cocktail and gently fold it to express the oils into the drink, then place the zest skin side up on the rim of the glass.

We use specific terms to refer to the width and length of a citrus zest garnish.

TWISTS are long and skinny. Made by running a zester continuously around the equator of the citrus two times.

SWATHS are thicker and shorter than twists. Made by zesting straight down the length of the citrus, from stem end to blossom end.

LONG SWATHS are longer than regular swaths. Should be 3½ to 4 inches long.

HORSE'S NECKS are the longest citrus zest garnishes. Made by zesting an entire lemon in one long curl, beginning at the stem end and continuing around the fruit at an angle to remove the full zest. This garnish is used pretty much exclusively for crustas like the Creole Crusta (page 39).

Fresh herbs • Lightly press fresh herbs between your fingers to release their aromas just before garnishing. In drinks that have straws, we usually tuck the garnish next to the straw so that when someone takes a sip they smell the herb's aromas, enhancing the experience of drinking the cocktail. To garnish with fresh mint, we use the "crowns" of the sprigs, which is the top of the sprig, including the top 2 or 3 leaves.

Powdered sugar • Sprinkling powdered sugar over a cocktail contributes a light confectionary aroma. At Julep, we keep our powdered sugar in a shaker with a perforated top that makes it very easy to add a light dusting to a drink. For home use, I recommend using a fine strainer: Place a spoonful of sugar in the strainer bowl, hold it over the cocktail, and gently tap the edge of the bowl once or twice to add a light dusting of sugar.

Mist of bitters • In certain circumstances, a mister is a perfectly efficient way to use bitters, such as Angostura, Herbsaint, or absinthe. The mister distributes the bitters completely and efficiently either into a glass as a rinse or over a cocktail as a garnish. We use Misto sprayers; a glass atomizer is a good option for home use. Alternatively, use 2 or 3 dashes of bitters as garnish or ¼ ounce for rinsing the glass.

The Juleps

Naturally, I must begin with the Southern cocktail that inspires me so much I named my bar after it. The first julep was not the mint-sugar-bourbon concoction often presented today as the definitive julep. In fact, the earliest juleps, which were mixed in the late 1700s, could include pretty much any spirit. And so there were gin juleps, rum juleps, even madeira juleps. By the mid-1800s, many sources, including Jerry Thomas's seminal 1862 book, *The Bar-Tender's Guide*, asserted that the true Southern julep was mint, sugar, cognac, and peach brandy. What interests me more than the spirits the original julep was made with is the purpose: to mask and mellow bitter remedies, making them easier to ingest. This is implied in the etymology of the word *julep*. It comes from the Persian *golab*, or "rose water," an aromatic distillation of rose petals and water used as a medicine, cosmetic, and flavoring in food and drink. The julep was not incidental to medical care but was in fact a trusted treatment—one of many ways the history of alcohol intersects with the history of medicine. By the nineteenth century, the julep began to appear in books as a proper social drink.

The reason the julep became consistently associated with whiskey, especially bourbon, has a lot to do with the state of the American South a century and a half ago. Jerry Thomas wrote that the julep "in the Southern states is more popular than any other [drink]." However, one year into the Civil War nobody in the South was writing much on the topic of social drinking. And a cocktail of this kind would have been inaccessible for ordinary citizens. This most Southern of beverages was the drink of only the very rich. They alone could afford something so lavish, which depended on a reliable supply of ice (more expensive than milk and much more difficult to store) and lots of cognac and peach brandy. Ice was rarely available beyond the limits of the prosperous port cities. And all those elegant sterling silver cups certainly denote luxury.

The sure path to guarantee that something becomes a highly desirable status symbol is for it to be nearly impossible to acquire. And this may be what led to bourbon becoming so linked to the julep. Bourbon was accessible to people no matter their social or economic status. It was even used as currency, with its long shelf life likely making it a solid investment. These developments may have accelerated the use and prominence of bourbon in julep making. An unadulterated bourbon julep is so balanced and enjoyable that it's no wonder it has held sway over so many for so long. However, I don't want to detract from the other delectable ways to interpret the cocktail. Here are seven of my best juleps.

JULEP

Mint Julep

Barware Julep cup + straw   **Serving Ice** Crushed

When I'm working out the formula for a cocktail—whether it's an original or our version of a classic—I consider how the rate of dilution will affect the drinkability of that cocktail as it sits. With the julep, served with crushed ice and most often consumed during warm and humid months, I presume there will be a substantial amount of dilution over the time it takes to sip the drink. It's important that the drink be delicious from first to last sip. The trick is to make sure that the alcohol content (the strength of the drink) is sufficient to stand up to that dilution over time but not so strong that it knocks the drinker over the head and makes it unwise to consider having a second. The ideal spirit for this julep is a mid-80s- to 90-proof bourbon. A straight 80 proof might drink well for the first few minutes, but as the ice begins to melt it will quickly become too diluted to be enjoyable. And a 100-proof bourbon has too much kick up front, so it risks dulling the taste buds (and diminishes the drinker's ability to consume more than one).

10 mint leaves

½ ounce Turbinado Syrup (page 192)

2 ounces mid-80s- to 90-proof bourbon

GARNISH

2 or 3 mint sprigs

Powdered sugar

Place the mint leaves and syrup in the julep cup and lightly press with a muddler. Leave the muddler in the glass and add the bourbon, pouring it over the muddler to rinse it off. Stir with the muddler to mix. Fill the cup a little more than halfway with crushed ice, and stir with a barspoon 15 to 20 times. Add more ice to form a dome on top. Place the straw in the cup.

To garnish, press the mint sprigs between your fingers to release their aroma and tuck them into the ice next to the straw. Dust the mint sprigs with the powdered sugar (see page 11).

Georgia Mint Julep

Barware Rocks glass + straw   **Serving Ice** Crushed

When I read the esteemed Jerry Thomas's assertion that true Southern juleps were made from mint, sugar, cognac, and peach brandy, I wondered about the exact nature of that peach brandy. Good peach brandy was produced beginning in the late 1700s and became quite coveted. But it was expensive to produce and to buy, so it's difficult to believe that the masses were putting it in their julep cups. That consideration aside, because distillation of peach brandy essentially died out during Prohibition and wasn't revived until the last couple of decades, we'll never know what peach brandy actually tasted like in the early 1800s. This means that every Georgia Mint Julep since Prohibition has been an interpretation of what the bartender thought the original might have tasted like. But that doesn't mean an excellent projection isn't possible. And no self-respecting bar in the South—especially not one named Julep—could exist without its own version of this original regional cocktail. For our version, we skipped the peach brandy debate entirely by using a high-quality peach liqueur and cutting back on the sugar.

10 mint leaves

2 barspoons Turbinado Syrup (page 192)

1½ ounces cognac, such as Pierre Ferrand 1840

½ ounce peach liqueur, such as Mathilde Peche

GARNISH

2 or 3 mint sprigs

2 or 3 blackberries

1 orange slice

Powdered sugar

Place the mint leaves and the syrup in the rocks glass and lightly press with a muddler. Leave the muddler in the glass and add the cognac and peach liqueur, pouring them over the muddler to rinse it off. Stir with the muddler to mix. Fill the glass a little more than halfway with crushed ice and stir with a barspoon 15 to 20 times. Add more ice to form a dome on top. Place the straw in the glass.

To garnish, press the mint sprigs between your fingers to release their aroma and tuck them into the ice next to the straw. Place the blackberries next to the mint and hang the orange slice on the rim of the glass. Dust the mint sprigs with the powdered sugar (see page 11).

Rock 'n' Rye Julep

Barware Julep cup + straw   **Serving Ice** Crushed

The very first julep was a medium for medicine not a recreational drink. Though I imagine the drinker of this concoction enjoyed the pleasant feeling that washed over him as he sipped, whether he considered it remedy or libation. The history of mixing drinks is interwoven with the history of pharmaceuticals in countless ways. This formula is my way of revisiting the practice of getting medicine down smoothly in the form of a julep. The original rock and rye wasn't much more than a shot of rye poured over a piece of rock candy, but its medicinal uses were many. By the middle of the nineteenth century, bottled rock and rye was prescribed to combat all manner of ailments, including coughs, sore throats, and runny noses. Its curative powers were sufficiently impressive that distillers were permitted to continue producing it during Prohibition. I guess a spoonful of sugar really does help the medicine go down. The peach tea in the syrup used here contributes a nice flavor as well as some puckery tannins to counter the sweetness of the rock and rye.

10 mint leaves

½ ounce Peach Honey Syrup (recipe follows)

1 ounce 100-proof bonded rye whiskey

1 ounce Slow & Low rock and rye whiskey

2 dashes Peychaud's bitters

GARNISH

2 or 3 mint sprigs

Powdered sugar

Place the mint leaves and syrup in the julep cup and lightly press with a muddler. Leave the muddler in the glass and add the rye, rock and rye, and bitters, pouring them over the muddler to rinse it off. Stir with the muddler to mix. Fill the cup a little more than halfway with crushed ice, and stir with a barspoon 15 to 20 times. Add more ice to form a dome on top. Place the straw in the cup.

To garnish, press the mint sprigs between your fingers to release their aroma and tuck them into the ice next to the straw. Dust the mint sprigs with the powdered sugar (see page 11).

PEACH HONEY SYRUP

Makes about 1 cup (8 ounces)

You may use a different brand of tea than the one I call for, but be sure it's based on white—not black or green—tea.

1 peach-flavored white tea bag, such as Republic of Tea

½ cup boiling water

¾ cup honey

Place the tea bag and boiling water in a glass measuring cup or small mixing bowl. Cover with a small plate and let stand to steep for 5 minutes. Remove the bag, pressing out the excess liquid. Pour off some tea as necessary to bring the total amount to ¼ cup. If the tea has cooled significantly, heat it in the microwave until hot. Pour in the honey and stir until well combined. Let cool completely before using. Store in a covered container in the refrigerator for up to 1 week.

Spiced Julep

Barware Julep cup + straw   **Serving Ice** Crushed

As a general rule, when I include a classic cocktail on our menu, I stay as true to its original form as I can. Two of my favorite cocktails really tested this rule. First was the Jersey Lighthouse, built from sugar, Angostura bitters, cloves, lemon peel, and applejack, and then set on fire. It's fantastic and fun, but during our tests the cocktail glasses had an unfortunate habit of breaking when their contents were set aflame. (And in Houston, we have only about two and a half days a year when it's cold enough to warrant a flaming drink.) This got me thinking about another wintery classic that I love: the Tom and Jerry, a rich, creamy concoction laced with cloves, allspice, and cinnamon. Often made around the holidays, it's almost like warm eggnog—another one we could put on the menu for just a couple of days a year. I shelved these thoughts but pocketed two key elements—the fire of the Jersey Lighthouse and the warm spices of both drinks—for the time when something would inevitably prompt me to rethink the idea.

That time came when I began developing our selection of juleps. I knew for sure that I was looking for a few things: at least one unusual julep (the appealing and delicious confectionary notes that come from warm spices fit the bill); a drink that has a bright, punchy flavor without being a citrus-based punch; and a cocktail we can light on fire without the risk of exploding glassware. Eventually, these separate ideas merged into this single fabulous cocktail. The spices are placed in a mesh tea ball and soaked in overproof rum so that they easily catch fire, while the traditional metal julep cup ensures that the fire remains safely inside its boundaries. The order in which the ingredients are added ensures a cool spectacle and an incredible aroma. The flaming spices are placed in the cup with the mint and liquor. The Jamaican rum and orange zest are essential, contrasting the mint and pulling together the flavors of those warm spices. The flame is extinguished only when the crushed ice is added. The result is an exceptionally well-balanced drink with lovely, rounded caramel notes. The fire not only makes a great show, it also helps integrate each element by toasting the spices and concentrating the flavor of the liquor.

continued

Sparkling Julep

Barware Skinny collins glass + straw   **Serving Ice** Crushed

The first time I tasted a sparkling wine made with 100 percent Gamay grapes, my immediate thought was that it's an ideal cocktail ingredient. This red sparkling wine has enough character to hold its own in a mixed drink and yet is light enough to blend well with others. So when I decided to include a version of the classic champagne julep on our menu, I knew right away which sparkling wine I wanted to use. Granted, the Gamay doesn't have everything it needs to carry this julep—no sparkling wine does. One thing that often bothers me about champagne juleps is that they're so light they're almost not there. You can't let the ice soften and dilute the wine so much that the result is a bland version of a sparkling wine cooler. The mix needs structure, and for that we include a touch of cognac. It provides the backbone so the Gamay can shine in this ornate and refreshing julep.

10 mint leaves

½ ounce Turbinado Syrup (page 192)

¾ ounce cognac, preferably Pierre Ferrand 1840

2 ounces sparkling FRV100 Gamay, plus ½ ounce for topping off

GARNISH

2 or 3 mint sprigs

1 small bunch champagne or other tiny grapes

Powdered sugar

Place the mint leaves and syrup in the glass and lightly press with a muddler. Leave the muddler in the glass and add the cognac and 2 ounces of sparkling Gamay, pouring them over the muddler to rinse it off. Stir with the muddler to mix. Fill the glass a little more than halfway with crushed ice and stir with a barspoon 15 to 20 times. Add more ice to completely fill the glass. Top off with the remaining ½ ounce of sparkling Gamay. Place the straw in the glass.

To garnish, press the mint sprigs between your fingers to release their aroma and tuck them into the ice next to the straw. Place the champagne grapes alongside the mint and dust them with the powdered sugar (see page 11).

Honeysuckle Julep

Barware Julep cup + straw   **Serving Ice** Crushed

We throw a huge viewing party the first Saturday of every May to celebrate the Kentucky Derby. We bring in a local charity and host thousands of people throughout the day. In true Derby fashion, everyone dresses to the nines for the occasion, and we have best-hat and best-dressed contests, play games, and have a ball. We transform all of Julep, inside and out, into a flower garden, putting down turf and adorning every corner with flowers. One spring, the honeysuckle blooming all around Houston inspired us to create this julep especially for the Derby party.

10 mint leaves

½ ounce Honey Mix (page 195)

1¼ ounces vodka

¾ ounce Martine honeysuckle liqueur

¾ ounce coconut water

GARNISH

2 or 3 mint sprigs

1 blackberry

Half a lemon wheel

Powdered sugar

Place the mint leaves and honey mix in the julep cup and lightly press with a muddler. Leave the muddler in the glass and add the vodka, honeysuckle liqueur, and coconut water, pouring them over the muddler to rinse it off. Stir with the muddler to mix. Fill the cup a little more than halfway with crushed ice and stir with a barspoon 15 to 20 times. Add more ice to form a dome on top. Place the straw in the cup.

To garnish, press the mint sprigs between your fingers to release their aroma and tuck them into the ice next to the straw. Place the blackberry next to the mint and place the half lemon wheel on the glass rim. Dust the mint sprigs with the powdered sugar (see page 11).

First Sip

To me a cocktail isn't simply about balance and texture, although these are critical. What really matters is how it makes you feel or what it makes you remember. When we developed the Topps & Bottoms (page 42), for instance, in addition to aiming for a particular flavor we set out to remind the drinker of the experience of going to a baseball game. When drinking a Julep cocktail, I hope that when you take that first sip, hear the cocktail's story, or enjoy the space you're in, the experience unlocks a memory or creates an entirely new one. It won't be the same response for everyone. A drink that makes me think of my grandmother might evoke something entirely different for you. But I always aim to incite the memory or feeling of something.

How do you get someone to fall in love with a new concept? That was the question in the back of my mind when I created Julep's opening menu. I knew that, in many ways, the first sips taken were going to define the bar. It was exhilarating—and daunting. You get just one chance to make a first impression. I had spent years gathering flavors and testing cocktail after cocktail hundreds of times. Now I was going to present a collection that represented the culmination of all that. I wanted to talk about Southern ingredients, but not in the context of classic Southern dishes, and about what it means to be from the South, but not in an obvious or literal way. While the menus that followed our first one were thematic around history, that first menu needed to tell a story and demonstrate what *my* Southern bar was going to do. My team and I set out to reflect the modern Southern mentality and sensibilities.

So what makes the fourteen drinks in this chapter so special? We've been serving them ever since we opened. They are iconic to Julep. In fact, they are now listed on the menu as "House Favorites." They are exceptional because they are new and innovative and they feel Southern. They are unique but accessible and never overwhelming. They ease you in and tell you a story—or ready you to tell your own. They rely on new South ingredients, such as hard cider, as well as classic old South ingredients, like bourbon. Modern and traditional together—this is the state of the current South, and this is what drinking at Julep is all about.

Armagnac Sazerac

Barware 5.5-ounce cocktail coupe, chilled (see page 6)   **Serving ice** None

Many take it as gospel that the original Sazerac (page 152) was a cognac-based cocktail created in antebellum New Orleans. But the truth is elusive. Others say that the Sazerac morphed into a rye whiskey–based cocktail primarily because the phylloxera blight nearly obliterated France's wine- and grape-based spirits industry, drying up the cognac supply and forcing improvisation. Still others assert that the Sazerac was *always* a rye-based cocktail. Bits of each theory are supported by what we do know about New Orleans in the middle of the nineteenth century. The busy port city received shiploads of French spirits, so it's conceivable that cognac was in sufficient supply to inspire the cocktail—if indeed New Orleans is even its birth city. (Even this aspect of the story is debated in some circles, while in others the presence of absinthe is all that's needed to prove the Sazerac's Big Easy provenance.)

Wherever or from whatever it was born, a well-made Sazerac showcases all that's right with the classic cocktail's spirit-bitters-sugar-water formula, while its obscure origins inspire people like me to consider what other spirits might have appeared in its earliest incarnations—or might be used today. These musings led me to Armagnac, a more rustic style of brandy than cognac. The result was amazing, even before I tweaked the formula to adapt to Armagnac's austerity. That's where the barrel-aged Abbott's bitters come in: they are really important to round out the flavor.

Absinthe mist (page 11) or ¼ ounce absinthe, for rinsing the coupe	1 barspoon Turbinado Syrup (page 192)
	4 dashes Peychaud's bitters
1 ounce 100-proof bonded rye whiskey	2 dashes Abbott's bitters
1 ounce Armagnac, such as Marie Duffau Napoleon	**GARNISH**
	1 swath lemon zest

Mist the glass with the absinthe or pour in ¼ ounce absinthe and turn to coat the sides and bottom thoroughly. Set aside.

Pour the rye, Armagnac, syrup, Peychaud's bitters, and Abbott's bitters into a mixing glass. Fill the glass with ice cubes. Stir 20 times with a barspoon. Strain into the chilled glass.

Garnish with the lemon zest.

Oregano Cobbler

Barware Copper tumbler or other 10-ounce metal cup + straw   **Serving Ice** None

Cobblers are traditionally wine-based (particularly fortified wines like madeira and sherry) cocktails with fruit. They were extremely popular in the South in the 1800s, when both fortified wine and fruit were abundant, and the chipped ice they were served over was all the rage. Their low-alcohol profile makes them refreshing without packing a punch. I loved the idea of having a fruit-forward, session-style drink (see page 45) on Julep's opening menu, which made the cobbler a natural choice. Wanting to try something off the beaten path while staying true to the components of the cocktail, I used lemon as the fruit, added fresh oregano for a savory note, and played around with the wine base. I wanted something distinctive to go with the lemon and oregano, so I landed on bianco vermouth, with its bright notes, beautiful minerality, and balanced acidity. I initially made the cocktail with gin but changed it to mezcal because it called for a little more backbone. Feeling as if I needed a rationale to color outside the lines, I remembered my grandfather in Mexico calling all distilled spirits "vino." One aspect of being bilingual, multicultural, and an immigrant is that language and culture are fluid. So while I know that mezcal is a distilled spirit made from agave,

not a wine, I also know that it's referred to as wine in Mexico, and this fluidity gives me ideas. The mezcal and bianco vermouth play on each other's minerality. As I built this drink, all that was missing was a sweet component for balance, so I added a touch of sugar syrup. And there it was: a cocktail true to its origins yet thoroughly modern.

1 ounce Carpano Bianco vermouth	**¼ ounce freshly squeezed lemon juice**
1 ounce fino sherry	**2 fresh oregano sprigs**
¾ ounce mezcal	
¼ ounce Simple Syrup (page 193)	**GARNISH**
	2 or 3 oregano sprigs

Fill the copper tumbler with crushed ice.

Pour the vermouth, sherry, mezcal, syrup, and lemon juice into a cocktail shaker. Add the 2 oregano sprigs. Fill the shaker with ice cubes. Cover and shake vigorously 20 times. Fine-strain the cocktail into the tumbler. Place the straw in the tumbler.

To garnish, press the oregano sprigs between your fingers to release their aroma and tuck them into the crushed ice in the center of the top of the cocktail.

Creole Crusta

Barware 5.5-ounce cordial glass or champagne flute   **Serving ice** None

These days the word *cocktail* refers to nearly any alcoholic beverage–based mixed drink.

But there was a time when the word referred to a specific prototype of the genre: a mixture of sugar, bitters, spirits, and water—the old-fashioned, essentially. But before it became comfortable to put any mixed-spirit drink into a single cocktail basket, a rich variety of names rolled off Colonial American tongues as fluidly as the drinks flowed down their throats. There were "sangarees," "smashes," "slings," "cups," and "flips," among others. One thing all these varieties shared was the lack of any kind of flourish in the form of garnishes. Then came the Fancy Cocktail, which marked a turning point in the category as one of the earliest drinks to be adorned by a long strip of lemon peel. Upping the ante on visual effects was a related concoction, the Brandy Crusta. Purportedly invented in 1852 by bartender Joseph Santina at a New Orleans bar called The Jewel of the South, it was first recorded in print ten years later, in Jerry Thomas's *The Bar-Tender's Guide*. Original recipes for the crusta vary quite a bit, but a few components are consistent: brandy, orange liqueur, lemon, bitters, and, most notably, a sugar-encrusted rim. Served in a tall, narrow-stemmed glass with that sparkling rim and topped off with a strip of lemon, the crusta was one of the first cocktails to invite us to drink with our eyes. It's hard to look at it without thinking that something so pretty *must* be delicious.

The crusta's enticement of both eye and palate was all we needed to consider it for Julep's menu. But the drink's likely birthplace and time got us thinking about how we could use our version of it to talk about an integral yet excruciating part of the story of the South: the trade routes that carried slaves, crops, textiles, and manufactured goods from Africa and the Caribbean to America and Europe. The slave trade is at the root of innumerable Southern food and drink traditions. For instance, among the most popular crustas were those made with rum, much of which came into America via these trading routes. You don't need to look beyond the reason that Jamaican Demerara rum got here to discover how certain spices came to the United States and why foods such as benne seed were grown here. Brought over by African slaves, it was in their subsistence gardens that the tiny benne seeds first took root in America, where it eventually became highly valued as a nutritious and versatile food as well as a soil-improving, pest-preventing crop. So our crusta became an amalgam of a few of the interconnected ingredients from those

continued

Creole Crusta, continued

trading routes: Jamaican rum, a benne- and sugar-encrusted glass, and a touch of orange and spice inspired by Martinique's famous Creole Shrubb.

There is simply no way to talk about Southern traditions without recognizing the human hardships from which they arose. We just hope our beautiful, delicious Creole Crusta can help make the conversations about the past flow a bit more easily.

To prepare the glass, combine the toasted benne and sugar in a saucer or small shallow plate. Rub the outer rim of the glass with the lemon wedge. Roll the top edge of the glass in the mixture to fully coat the outer rim. Set the glass aside with the lemon zest.

Pour the rum, Creole Shrubb, syrup, lemon juice, and bitters into a cocktail shaker. Fill the shaker with ice cubes. Close and shake vigorously 20 times.

Fine-strain the cocktail into the crusted glass.

Garnish with the lemon zest.

GARNISH

½ cup toasted and cooled benne seeds (see Note)

½ cup turbinado sugar

1 lemon wedge, for dampening the glass

1 horse's neck lemon zest (page 11)

1½ ounces Demerara rum, such El Dorado 5-year

½ ounce Clément Creole Shrubb

½ ounce Turbinado Syrup (page 192)

¾ ounce freshly squeezed lemon juice

5 dashes Hella Bitters Smoked Chili Cocktail Bitters

Note Anson Mills (see Resources, page 205) are the only growers of authentic benne seed in America, but you can substitute sesame seeds in a pinch. To toast benne seeds: Preheat the oven to 350°F. Spread the benne seeds on a rimmed baking sheet. Toast, stirring often, until the seeds are lightly browned and fragrant, 3 to 5 minutes. Transfer to a plate to cool.

You'll have enough of the benne and sugar combination to crust 4 to 6 glasses; store any left over in a tightly covered container for up to 1 month.

Topps & Bottoms

Julep's official opening day was August 3, 2014, at the height of baseball season. So we made it our goal to develop a cocktail for the opening menu that would capture the feeling of a long, leisurely summer afternoon spent cheering on the home team ("Go 'Stros!"). We wanted a throwback to the time you could buy a bag of roasted sunflower seeds for fifty cents, snag a pack of baseball cards for a buck, and settle into cheap seats at the Astrodome on a weeknight. The salty, bold, well-rounded Topps & Bottoms is the result. At Julep, we serve this cocktail with a small pouch of roasted sunflower seeds clipped to the glass (what would a baseball game be without them, for players and spectators alike?) and a Topps baseball card as a coaster. Batter up!

1½ ounces Sunflower Seed–Infused Overproof Rum (recipe follows)

1 ounce quinquina, such as Byrrh Grand Quinquina

½ ounce pamplemousse rose liqueur

GARNISH

Paper pouch (see Note)

Roasted, salted sunflower seed kernels

Tiny clothespin (no larger than 1-inch long)

Topps baseball card, for a coaster

Pour the rum, quinquina, and rose liqueur into a mixing glass. Fill the glass with ice cubes. Stir 20 times with a barspoon. Strain into the chilled glass.

To garnish, fill the paper pouch with some sunflower seeds and use the clothespin to attach it and the baseball card to the rim of the glass. Once served, the baseball card can be removed and used as a coaster.

Note If you ever played table football with your friends in middle school you already know how to make these little pouches. If not, here's how: Place a 4 by 3-inch piece of parchment paper on a surface with the long end facing you. Fold the two short sides into the center so that the edges of the paper meet in the middle. Fold the paper in half again at that centerline to form a rectangle that is roughly 1 inch wide by 3 inches long. Grasp the bottom corner on the open-edged side and fold it up to the opposite side to form a triangle shape. Pull the tip of the triangle up and fold it so that the bottom is squared off. Continue to fold the triangle up in this way twice more. Pinch the bottom closed tip and open the pouch at the top for filling.

continued

SUNFLOWER SEED–INFUSED OVERPROOF RUM

Makes 1 liter

It's important to pour the rum over the kernels while they're still hot, so that the flavor of the sunflower seeds is fully released into the rum.

2 cups raw, unsalted sunflower seed kernels

1 liter overproof aged rum, preferably Plantation Overproof

Preheat the oven to 350°F. Spread the sunflower seed kernels on a rimmed baking sheet. Toast, stirring often, until the kernels are evenly lightly browned and smell fragrant, 3 to 5 minutes.

Transfer the kernels to a 2-quart glass measuring cup or other glass container and pour the rum over the hot kernels. (Reserve the empty bottle if you'd like to store the infused rum in it.) Stir.

Loosely cover the container and let stand for 2 hours, stirring every 30 minutes.

Strain the rum through a strainer into a clean container and discard the kernels. Line the strainer with 2 layers of cheesecloth and strain the mixture 2 to 3 more times to remove all the particles. You can use the same cheese-cloth each time.

Transfer the infused rum to the reserved bottle or another container with a tight-fitting lid. Store in a cool place for up to 1 month.

Saint's Gallery

Barware 5.5-ounce cocktail coupe, chilled (see page 6)   **Serving ice** None

This cocktail was created in the spirit of session drinking, the practice of consuming low-alcohol drinks so that you can enjoy a long period of conviviality and imbibing while remaining socially acceptable. It's a custom that in some places has been elevated to an art form—which naturally brings us to New Orleans. It also brings us to a liqueur called Herbsaint that was invented in the city and is the source of this cocktail's name. Created after Prohibition by J. Marion Legendre, who had learned how to make anise-flavored absinthe in France during the First World War, Herbsaint was initially called Legendre Absinthe. It was presented as a stand-in for authentic absinthe, which had been outlawed because of fears that wormwood (the herb that gave the spirit its signature bitterness) was dangerously addictive and caused hallucinations and psychotic episodes. Never mind that Legendre Absinthe didn't contain wormwood: the liquor control arm of the U.S. government compelled Legendre to change the name of his creation to avoid any confusion. And so it was rechristened Herbsaint. This cocktail can be made with either Herbsaint or the again-legal absinthe (reports of its deleterious effects were highly overstated). The former yields a more lush result than the astringent absinthe.

Herbsaint mist (page 11) or ¼ ounce Herbsaint liqueur, for rinsing the coupe

1½ ounces Carpano Bianco vermouth

¾ ounce The Famous Grouse Smoky Black scotch (see Note)

½ ounce Bénédictine liqueur

Mist the glass with the Herbsaint or pour ¼ ounce Herbsaint into it and turn to coat the sides and bottom thoroughly. Set aside.

Pour the vermouth, scotch, and Bénédictine into a mixing glass. Fill the glass with ice cubes. Stir 20 times with a barspoon. Strain into the chilled glass.

Note The Famous Grouse Smoky Black scotch was formerly called The Black Grouse scotch.

Bottled in Bond

Barware 4 rocks glasses   **Serving ice** 4 (2-inch) cubes, plus crushed for the wine bucket

This Southern riff on the Manhattan is named after the label first put on some American-made whiskeys in the late nineteenth century. Until then, there had been no production or bottling standards for whiskey. Producers were free to water down or otherwise adulterate the whiskey they sold with impunity. Without fear of repercussion, they often added sugar, tea, or other flavorings to mask inferior quality, or they stretched their yield by adding water or moonshine. Then the Feds stepped in with the Bottled-in-Bond Act of 1897, passed with the help of producers like E. H. Taylor, eager for the tax incentives offered in exchange for much tighter restrictions on what they made and sold. The act dictated how and where spirits were distilled and bottled. Those produced according to these mandates were labeled "bottled in bond." We borrowed the name for this cocktail because we love the story of how the spirits industry was forced to clean up its act. Our good friend, Master Distiller Dave Pickerell, great-grandnephew of Col. E. H. Taylor, defines all bottled in bond spirits as bottled at 100 proof, from a single distillery during a single distillation season, and rested in oak barrels for a minimum of four years.

We present the bottled in bond to groups of four and serve it with small dishes of accompaniments that go beautifully with the drink: bourbon-infused cherries, dark chocolate, and roasted Marcona almonds.

6 ounces 100-proof bonded bourbon

6 ounces Cocchi vermouth di Torino

3 ounces 80-proof bourbon

1 ounce Carpano Antica Formula vermouth

5 ounces filtered water

¾ ounce Turbinado Syrup (page 192)

3 barspoons Angostura bitters

1 barspoon Abbott's bitters

GARNISH

Drained cherries from House Cherry Bounce (page 54)

High-quality dark chocolate (65% cacao or higher)

Roasted and salted Marcona almonds, with skins

In a 2-liter glass measuring cup or other container, combine the bonded bourbon, Torino, 80-proof bourbon, Carpano, water, syrup, Angostura bitters, and Abbott's bitters. Transfer to a 25-ounce decanter.

Place 1 ice cube in each of the 4 glasses. In 3 separate small dishes, place the strained cherries, the chocolate, and the almonds. Set the glasses and the dishes on a tray or table. Serve the decanter in a wine bucket filled with crushed ice.

Rail to Satsuma

Barware Collins glass + straw   **Serving ice** Crushed

This drink is our homage to the neighborhood where Julep is located—an area to the west of downtown Houston known as the Old Sixth Ward. Established in 1877, the Sixth Ward has a couple of notable features. First, its major thoroughfare, Washington Avenue (the street where Julep sits) was the western route to busy Washington County and its county seat, Washington-on-the-Brazos, a former capital of Texas where the Texas Declaration of Independence was signed in 1836. And second, it was the major hub for the Houston and Texas Central Railway's railroad lines that passed through Houston.

The remnants of this history are ever present, from the still-active railroad lines to the beautiful old Victorian houses, once owned by prosperous traders and merchants who profited from the proximity to the train routes and built alongside the modest homes that housed the railway workers. From its earliest days, the city of Houston had a tradition of people living in the areas where they worked, and many neighborhoods were developed with a medley of houses built for the affluent and working class alike. To this day, Houston is one of the most diverse cities in the country—one of the many reasons I love it.

Along the train route between Houston and Washington County was an area called Satsuma, named for the mandarin orange groves that developers intended to plant in abundance. That part of the plan never panned out, and Satsuma never became an official town—but among locals the name lingers. Those Satsumas were the first thing that came to mind when we started developing a fresh orange cocktail for the opening menu.

1 ounce cognac, such as Pierre Ferrand 1840

¾ ounce Satsuma Jelly (page 201)

½ ounce freshly squeezed lime juice

½ ounce Turbinado Syrup (page 192)

1 ounce India pale ale, such as More Cowbell IPA, for topping off

GARNISH

Half an orange wheel

2 or 3 mint sprigs

Fill the collins glass with crushed ice. Pour the cognac, jelly, lime juice, and syrup into a cocktail shaker. Fill the shaker with ice cubes. Cover and shake vigorously 20 times. Add the beer to the shaker. Strain into the glass. Place the straw in the glass.

To garnish, place the half orange wheel on the glass rim. Press the mint sprigs between your fingers to release their aroma and tuck them into the ice next to the orange.

Cider & Milk Punch

Barware Fat collins glass + straw   **Serving ice** Crushed

Nestled in the Great Smoky Mountains in East Tennessee is a place called Blackberry Farm, which encompasses many things across 4,200 glorious acres, including an award-winning restaurant, a luxurious resort, a fully working farm, an heirloom garden, a breathtakingly extensive wine cellar, and incredible people. I've been lucky to visit a few times to talk about the history and craft of making cocktails. On a trip there for an event celebrating women in food, wine, and music, I stayed in a cabin called Milk & Cider. Not realizing that it was named after an heirloom bean, I believed it was fate that I ended up in a cabin that sounded like the name of a drink. So I went for it. Combining the two ingredients in the bean-cabin's name, I quickly landed on the structure that became the cocktail: a classic Southern milk-and-whiskey punch based on a generous shot of hard cider.

2 ounces hard cider, preferably Foggy Ridge

½ ounce 100-proof bonded rye whiskey

¾ ounce half-and-half

¾ ounce Turbinado Syrup (page 192)

1 egg white

GARNISH

Whole nutmeg

Fill the glass with crushed ice. Pour the cider, rye, half-and-half, syrup, and egg white into a cocktail shaker. Cover and dry shake vigorously 20 times. Open and fill the shaker with ice cubes. Cover and shake vigorously 40 times. Strain into the glass. Place the straw in the glass.

Garnish with a few grates of nutmeg.

Cherry Bounce Sour

Barware Skinny collins glass   **Serving ice** 4 (1¼-inch) cubes, or as needed

This cocktail is so popular that from the time I first introduced it on our opening night, I've never taken it off the menu. It's based on a centuries-old method of preserving cherries in sugar, spices, and spirits. This method enabled people to keep fresh cherries long past their season, for pies or compotes, and created a delicious, boozy cordial called the "bounce." George Washington apparently loved cherry bounce so much that he carried a canteen of it—along with madeira and port—when he took a trip across the Allegheny Mountains in 1784. I can understand his enthusiasm: it's worth every day of waiting for the mixture to be ready to drink. And while I agree with President Washington that the bounce is good enough to drink on its own, I love it even more in the form of a bourbon sour.

2 ounces House Cherry Bounce (recipe follows)

1½ ounces 100-proof bonded bourbon

1 ounce freshly squeezed lemon juice

¾ ounce Turbinado Syrup (page 192)

1 egg white

1 dash Angostura bitters

GARNISH

Angostura mist (see page 11) or 3 dashes Angostura bitters

Place the 4 ice cubes in the glass, adding more if needed to fill the glass halfway.

Pour the cherry bounce, bourbon, lemon juice, syrup, egg white, and 1 dash Angostura bitters into a cocktail shaker. Cover and dry shake vigorously 20 times. Open and fill the shaker with ice cubes. Cover and shake vigorously 40 times. Strain into the glass. To garnish, spray Angostura mist 1 time over the surface of the cocktail or add 3 dashes of bitters.

continued

HOUSE CHERRY BOUNCE

Makes about 1 quart

This process produces two delicious items: A boozy fruit bounce, of course, and bourbon cherries that can be eaten however you like. We serve them with the Bottled in Bond (page 49) and as an accompaniment to our cheese board.

3½ pounds Bing cherries

1 cup Sugar in the Raw turbinado

2 (2-inch) cinnamon sticks

1 or 2 whole cloves

1 small star anise

½ nutmeg (see Note)

1¼ cups 100-proof bonded bourbon

Pit the cherries into a bowl to collect the juice as well as the fruit; discard the pits. Gently press the fruit with a muddler or large spoon (this is just to release a little juice; you don't want to break up the cherries).

Transfer the cherries and their juice to a saucepan. Stir in the sugar, cinnamon sticks, clove(s), star anise, and nutmeg. Cook over medium-low heat, stirring constantly, for 20 minutes, until the sugar dissolves.

Remove from the heat and let cool.

Line a strainer set over a bowl with cheesecloth. Strain the cherry mixture through the cheesecloth. Remove and discard the cinnamon sticks, nutmeg, and clove. Transfer the cherries to an airtight container and store in the refrigerator for up to 1 week.

Transfer the strained juice to a 1-quart canning jar. Add the bourbon. Cover the jar tightly and refrigerate for 2 to 3 weeks before using. Continue to store in the refrigerator for up to 3 months.

Note Whole nutmeg is very easy to cut in half with a chef's knife.

Stone Fence Sour

Barware 13.25-ounce glass + straw   **Serving ice** Crushed

It is said that Ethan Allen and his gang of Green Mountain Boys first concocted the Stone Fence, a hard cider–and–rum libation, the night before they joined forces with Benedict Arnold and his men to seize Fort Ticonderoga from the British in 1775. The many tons of cannon taken from this critical throughway on the southern end of Lake Champlain were painstakingly transported to Boston, where they had a lot to do with persuading the British to evacuate the city.

What's always caught my attention about this anecdote is that the name Stone Fence—a drink a bunch of rowdy colonials used for liquid courage—reminds me of something else entirely. When I first began bartending back in 2000, one of the more popular drinks was a Stone Sour, made from a base (whiskey, vodka, amaretto, or whatever the guest chose), powdered sweet-and-sour mix, and orange juice from a bottle. At the first bar I worked, I must have served hundreds of Amaretto Stone Sours every weekend.

So here's the Stone Fence Sour, offering hints of both the Stone Sour and the Stone Fence: dry apple notes, a whiskey backbone, and a balanced sweet-and-sour element. It's strong enough to give you courage no matter what you're planning for tomorrow.

1½ ounces 80-proof bourbon

1½ ounces hard cider, preferably Foggy Ridge

½ ounce orgeat

½ ounce Simple Syrup (page 193)

½ ounce freshly squeezed lime juice

½ ounce freshly squeezed orange juice

GARNISH

3 apple slices

Whole nutmeg

Pour the bourbon, hard cider, orgeat, syrup, lime juice, and orange juice into the glass. Stir with a barspoon to blend. Fill the glass halfway with crushed ice and stir a few times. Fill the glass entirely with crushed ice. Place the straw in the glass. To garnish, thread the apple slices on a cocktail pick and place on the rim of the glass. Add a few grates of nutmeg.

Comstock Toddy

Barware Toddy glass or an 8-ounce heatproof glass

Serving ice None

My favorite theory about how rainwater madeira got its name is that a shipment of regular madeira from Portugal was left out in the rain at the port of Savannah, became diluted and slightly salinized, and was passed off by unscrupulous merchants as a new style of the prized fortified wine to hapless Southern consumers. They loved it so much that the demand for this inferior product skyrocketed. A good friend of mine, who is a chemistry professor at Rice University, pointed out that the breaching of so many bottles by rainwater would lead not only to a lighter product but also to a degree of contamination that would make a lot of people very sick. It's not that I believed the story, but that I'm amazed by how many stories about the South hinge on the stereotype of Southerners as universally dense. While it's true that rainwater madeira became widely popular in the South, I don't believe that thousands of thickheaded Georgians were hoodwinked. I think it was because this lighter style of madeira is especially pleasing when the temperature and humidity are high, and it is an excellent and versatile blending alcohol for cocktails of any temperature. In this toddy, for example, the rainwater madeira and the apricot liqueur soften the harsher edges of the bourbon and set it up to be as smooth and soothing as a warm hug on a cold winter night.

1½ ounces 80-proof bourbon

¾ ounce apricot liqueur

½ ounce rainwater madeira

¾ ounce Honey Mix (page 195)

4 ounces Hot Cinnamon Tea (page 199)

3 saffron threads

GARNISH

1 swath lemon zest

1 star anise

Pour the bourbon, liqueur, madeira, and honey mix in the glass and stir with a barspoon to blend. Add the hot tea and saffron threads and stir.

To garnish, lay a cocktail pick across the rim of the glass and rest the lemon zest and star anise on it.

Tequila Toddy

When I was a kid, my mom used to give me and my siblings mugs of hot cinnamon tea at the end of the day to settle our stomachs and ease us into sleep. At least that was her hope—she rarely had luck with me, a natural-born night owl. Until I became an adult, I assumed that drinking cinnamon tea before bed was a Southern tradition. Then it dawned on me that this habit more likely came from our original Mexican roots than from our transplanted Southern ones.

It also occurred to me that hot cinnamon tea would be a brilliant replacement for the plain hot water that is one of the pillars of a classic hot toddy (in addition to alcohol and sugar). Flavorings such as lemon and spices are often added to bump up the taste and aroma of toddies, but they can't compensate for the plain hot water that really dilutes the drink. However, when you infuse that hot water with fragrant cinnamon, you add an unexpected—and unexpectedly delicious—element. I tried it once, and every toddy I've made since then is based on a hot cinnamon tea or other infusion, rather than plain hot water.

That's how I discovered that cinnamon and tequila are absolutely made for each other. Now, I know that some people hear what's in this toddy and wonder whether *hot* tequila is something they could—or should—ever want. I love disrupting people's expectations by proposing something that sounds like it could possibly be a mistake. There's definitely no mistake here. The baked agave notes from a 100 percent agave tequila complement the warm flavor and aroma of the cinnamon infusion, and Pedro Ximénez sherry adds a raisin-like, confectionary quality. It's a sultry hot toddy, perfect for a cold night—an entirely grown-up way to ease into the end of the day.

1½ ounces Tequila Ocho Plata

½ ounce Pedro Ximénez sherry, such as El Candado

½ ounce Turbinado Syrup (page 192)

3 ounces Hot Cinnamon Tea (page 199)

GARNISH

1 cinnamon stick

1 lemon twist

Pour the tequila, sherry, and syrup into the glass and stir to blend. Add the hot tea.

To garnish, lay the cinnamon stick across the rim of the glass and drape the lemon twist over it.

Sassafras Punch

Barware Rocks glass   **Serving ice** 1¼-inch cubes

Sassafras has been utilized as both food and medicine for centuries. Native Americans and European settlers used sassafras root and bark as a curative. Its leaves are dried and ground to make filé powder, used to thicken and season gumbo, a Creole stew. Sassafras is the defining flavor (and was once the defining ingredient) in root beer. Just as the cinnamon tea I use in hot toddies speaks to my Mexican heritage, sassafras tea resonates with my Southern identity. I know I'm not the only Southerner who feels nostalgic about it. A couple of years ago I created all the cocktails for the Pop South Southern Foodways Alliance Symposium in Oxford, Mississippi, where celebrated Charleston chef Sean Brock and his mom, Renee, prepared the Saturday luncheon. Sean's only request for the cocktail I made to pair with his meal was that it include sassafras tea.

When building a cocktail around an ingredient like sassafras tea, the main factors to consider are that the tea is water-based (already diluted) and that the base flavor is delicate. To achieve perfect balance in the drink, it's important that it is not overly diluted (especially after adding ice) and that the other elements are simple. Nothing should overwhelm the subtle flavor you're trying to highlight. The Sassafras Punch has only a few ingredients and is designed to stay balanced over time—thanks to what lies hidden in the beautiful garnish. A little parcel tucked into the drink evokes a sassafras tea bag but actually holds a sugar cube. As the drink sits and the ice melts, the structure of the cocktail stays strong because the sugar slowly dissolves to maintain that lovely balance.

"What grows together goes together" is a common refrain in the culinary world. In other words, ingredients from the same region are generally compatible. This is apparent in both the Tequila Toddy (page 60), where I channeled my Mexican roots to pair cinnamon with tequila, and the Sassafras Punch, where two Southern traditions—sassafras and bourbon— go together beautifully. Crafting great cocktails, like so many things in life, often depends on being mindful of your past while forging your future.

continued

GARNISH

1 sugar cube

2 or 3 mint sprigs

1½ ounces mid-80s-
to 90-proof bourbon

¾ ounce Sassafras
Tea (page 200)

¾ ounce freshly
squeezed lemon juice

½ ounce maple syrup

To prepare the "tea bag" garnish, have ready a 2-inch square of cheesecloth, a 6-inch length of thin kitchen string, a 1 by 2-inch piece of heavy plain paper, and a stapler. Place the sugar cube for the garnish in the cheesecloth and tie it closed with the string. Fold the piece of paper over the loose end of the string and staple to secure it in place.

Place the "tea bag" in the glass so that the tagged end hangs out of it (as it would in a cup of tea) and fill the glass with ice cubes. Set aside.

Pour the bourbon, Sassafras Tea, lemon juice, and syrup into a cocktail shaker. Fill the shaker with ice cubes. Cover and shake vigorously 20 times. Strain into the glass.

Press the mint sprigs between your fingers to release their aroma and tuck them into the glass near the tea bag.

The Rural South

In February 2015, we launched a series of three menus to explore Southern heritage through cocktails. I wanted to take a full year to tell some real stories of the South. I knew that by the end of the year, we'd be talking about the Civil War, but I didn't want to begin there.

So we began gently. We set out to explore the rural South in a way that allowed us to be creative and enlightening while keeping it lighthearted. In this menu, we utilized ingredients native to the South's rural regions in order to tell a story of resourcefulness and perseverance— aspects of Southern identity that are inherently valuable yet often overlooked or dismissed. Some people may think the term *Rural South* refers to some place that existed long ago. And there are definitely elements of the past in these drinks. The Snake-bit Sprout (page 69), for example, tells the story of using chamomile topically as a folk remedy to keep the venom from a snake bite from spreading too quickly. But the Rural South absolutely hasn't disappeared. This menu was about exploring what it means today and moving beyond the stereotypes that exist around the term. I wanted the drinks to open up discussions about what life is like in towns with a population of fifteen hundred people. How do we talk about these places? On my way to Oxford, Mississippi, I probably pass through twenty towns like these. I yearned to create a forum where people could consider this part of the South in ways that avoid simple answers yet remain appealing. In my view, this is where you'll find the most interesting stories and the most captivating people.

Snake-bit Sprout

Glassware Collins glass + straw   **Serving ice** 4 (1¼-inch) cubes, plus crushed ice for the top layer

Wherever there's a dearth of advanced medicine, people will rely on traditional remedies and knowledge passed down through the generations. That was certainly the reality in many areas of the rural South. One of the folk cures we learned about while doing research for this menu is that a tincture of chamomile was used to soothe all sorts of skin injuries, including snakebites. I loved the idea of a chamomile-based cocktail. The first challenge was figuring out how best to get that subtle, floral flavor to shine through. We decided to infuse spirits with dried chamomile flowers and tried several varieties before settling on gin. From there, we built around that base. During the final stages of perfecting the cocktail, I recalled the Snakebite: a beer drink made by filling a pint glass halfway with hard cider and layering a stout on top. (Some people think of snakes when they hear about snakebites, but I think of drinking something delicious.) I had the idea to incorporate layering, and the result is the layered Snake-bit Sprout—dry, tart, and a little sweet. It might not cure you if you get bitten by a snake, but it'll certainly help you pass the time.

1½ ounces Chamomile-Infused London Dry Gin (recipe follows)

½ ounce freshly squeezed lime juice

½ ounce fresh pineapple juice (see Note)

½ ounce Simple Syrup (page 193)

1½ ounces hard cider, preferably Foggy Ridge

GARNISH

Dried chamomile buds

Fill the glass with the 4 ice cubes, or slightly more than halfway. Pour the gin, lime juice, pineapple juice, and syrup into a cocktail shaker. Fill the shaker with ice cubes. Cover and shake vigorously 20 times. Strain into the glass. Add crushed ice to reach the top of the glass. Top off with the cider. Place the straw in the glass.

Garnish with a few chamomile buds.

Note   For this cocktail, we used freshly juiced pineapple. If you don't have a juicer, use the highest quality fresh pineapple juice you can find. It's sometimes found in the refrigerated sections of produce departments. Store fresh pineapple juice in the refrigerator for up to 3 days. Avoid canned, shelf-stable juice, which can taste metallic.

continued

CHAMOMILE-INFUSED LONDON DRY GIN

Makes 1 liter

You can buy dried chamomile buds in bulk from health food stores, some tea shops, and online.

1 liter London dry gin

1 ounce dried chamomile buds

Combine the gin and chamomile in a 2-quart glass measuring cup or other container. (Reserve the empty gin bottle if you'd like to store the infused gin in it.) Cover and let stand for 3 hours.

Line a mesh strainer set over a bowl with cheesecloth. Strain the gin through the cheesecloth. Discard the chamomile. Transfer the infused gin to the reserved bottle or another container with a tight-fitting lid. Store in a cool place for up to 1 month. (We always use it up in that time.) You can store it longer, but the chamomile flavor will begin to fade.

Cajun Fig Soda

Glassware Rocks glass   **Serving ice** 1¼-inch cubes

Native to China, kumquats were originally brought to the Antebellum South by way of Europe and were soon planted widely. They were one of the few citrus fruits that could be cultivated as far north as the Florida Panhandle and Louisiana. With their pleasing sweet-and-sour flavor and fully edible peel, kumquats are widely used in Cajun and Creole cuisine. One of our farmers in Louisiana calls them Cajun figs. A name like that deserves to be memorialized.

Inspired by old-fashioned cream soda, this is essentially an orange cream soda highball. With rum providing the structure, the orange flavor is delivered through homemade kumquat syrup, and the creamy element comes from a barspoon of half-and-half, underscored by the crucial addition of Bittermens Orange Citrate (see page 8).

1½ ounces Demerara rum, such as El Dorado 5-year

½ ounce Kumquat Syrup (recipe follows)

1 barspoon freshly squeezed lime juice

1 barspoon half-and-half

2 dashes Bittermens Orange Citrate

Soda water, for topping off

GARNISH

2 mint sprigs

1 Dried Orange Wheel (recipe follows)

Fill the glass with ice cubes. Pour the rum, syrup, lime juice, half-and-half, and orange cream citrate into a cocktail shaker. Fill the shaker with ice cubes. Cover and shake vigorously 20 times. Strain into the glass. Top off with soda water.

Press the mint sprigs between your fingers to release their aroma. Push the sprigs through the center of the dried orange wheel and place on top of the cocktail.

continued

KUMQUAT SYRUP

Makes about 1½ cups (12 ounces)

Simmering tiny whole kumquats with an equal volume of sugar and water for a long time results in a lush, citrusy syrup with tart undertones.

1 cup whole kumquats	**1 cup water**
1 cup granulated sugar	

Place the kumquats, sugar, and water in a saucepan and stir to combine. Bring to a simmer over low heat and simmer gently, uncovered, for 2 hours, stirring frequently.

Strain the syrup, pressing on the kumquats to extract as much liquid as possible; discard the kumquats. Store the syrup in a covered container in the refrigerator for up to 2 weeks.

DRIED ORANGE WHEELS

Makes about 8 wheels

You can find dried orange slices in stores and online, but they are expensive, especially considering that you can easily produce beautiful dried orange wheels with very little effort and at a fraction of the price. We use a dehydrator at Julep, as you surely will if you have one. If not, the oven works perfectly. The total number of pretty wheels you get from an orange will vary; we typically get between 8 and 12 usable wheels per orange at Julep.

1 small orange, sliced crosswise into ½-inch-thick wheels, seeds removed	**Powdered sugar, for dusting**

Preheat the oven to 200°F. Line a baking sheet with parchment paper. Arrange the orange wheels in a single layer on the lined baking sheet. Dust the wheels lightly with the powdered sugar.

Bake for 1 hour. Remove the wheels from the oven and use a spatula to turn them over. Return the pan to the oven and bake until the wheels are dry and translucent, 1 to 1½ hours.

Let the wheels cool completely on the baking sheet.

To store the wheels, pour a 1-inch layer of dry rice into a canning jar with a tight-fitting lid. Cover the rice with a layer of cheesecloth. Stack the orange slices in the jar and cover tightly. Store at room temperature for up to 2 weeks.

French Camp Post

Glassware 7.5-ounce cocktail coupe, chilled (see page 6)   **Serving ice** None

This cocktail is named for a rural Mississippi town with a population of 174. In 1810, frontiersman and trader Louis LeFleur established a trading post and inn along the Natchez Trace, the trading route that led from Nashville, Tennessee, to Natchez, Mississippi, on the Mississippi River. A town grew around LeFleur's post, which became known as Frenchman's Camp by European explorers, American settlers, and the local Choctaw and Chickasaw tribes. Now called French Camp, the original shotgun-style post office still stands, complete with the front porch that would have been the epicenter of social life in this once-bustling town. This bold and alluring cocktail evokes the true grit of rural Southern towns like French Camp by shunning unnecessary embellishments in favor of delicious simplicity.

Pineau des Charantes is made by combining slightly fermented red, white, or rosé grape juice with cognac; some Pineaux are then barrel-aged together. It's popular in France, especially in the Charentes region where it is made. It's delicious served slightly chilled on its own, and it makes a remarkably good blending spirit in cocktails, contributing rusticity along with a nice, sweet-acid balance. I recommend Pierre Ferrand's Pineau des Charantes, a good option that is widely available.

1 ounce 110- to 120-proof bourbon

1 ounce white Pineau des Charantes, such as Pierre Ferrand

1 ounce kina, such as Kina l'Avion d'Or

1 drop vanilla extract

Pour the bourbon, Pineau des Charantes, Kina l'Avion d'Or, and vanilla into a mixing glass. Fill the glass with ice cubes. Stir 20 times with a barspoon. Strain into the chilled glass.

Two Drinks Coming

Barware Rocks glass + straw   **Serving ice** Crushed

Like many of the world's great inventions, this cocktail evolved from an oversight. For our Friends and Family Night, we invited guests to come in and help us practice being in the space for the first time, to discover what needed tweaking before opening night. This included printing the menu—ideally after a careful proofread. But we missed that part, so that night's menu listed "Two drinks coming" instead of the two cocktails that were still under construction. The typo must have been eye-catching because we kept having to explain that it wasn't a real drink and, no, we couldn't make it. After that night, I felt obliged to invent the Two Drinks Coming.

When we were brainstorming our Rural South menu, one of the bartenders joked that "you can't get much more country than SoCo and lime." For the uninitiated, *SoCo* stands for Southern Comfort, a bottled liqueur that tastes of fruit and spiced bourbon—although most of it hasn't been made with whiskey for years. We started thinking about the liqueur's origins. Southern Comfort is based on a cocktail invented by M. W. Heron, a New Orleans bartender who improved the harsh, almost undrinkable, subpar whiskey (prevalent in the nineteenth century) by infusing it with fruit and

spices. He dubbed his agreeable cocktail Cuffs and Buttons. We saw potential in M. W. Heron's original formula, so we played around by infusing bourbon with dried fruit and spices, and we developed our own house SoCo.

I'd recently read in *Bon Appétit* about the way Chef Yotam Ottolenghi uses sun-dried limes in his cooking. These are made by boiling fresh limes or lemons in salt brine and then drying them in the sun until they harden. A staple in some Middle Eastern cuisines, they're used to add unique flavor and aroma to soups and stews. In Houston, one of the most diverse cities in America, I found dried limes right up the street and used them to make an incredible lime cordial. (Check out Middle Eastern markets near you [see Resources, page 205].)

Together, the house SoCo and the lime cordial made a delicious cocktail. Now all we had to do was figure out how to keep the cocktail true to its name and fit two drinks into a single glass. So we borrowed from Tiki culture and used a spent lime shell as a shot glass.

continued

1 ounce House
"SoCo" Bourbon
(recipe follows)

1 ounce Lime Cordial
(page 196)

¼ ounce freshly
squeezed lime juice,
lime shells reserved

GARNISH

½ lime shell

½ ounce House
"SoCo" Bourbon
(recipe follows)

Fill the glass with crushed ice. Pour the "SoCo," cordial, and lime juice into a cocktail shaker. Fill the shaker with ice cubes. Cover and shake vigorously 20 times. Strain into the glass and place the straw in the glass.

To garnish, pour ½ ounce "SoCo" into a juiced lime shell and place it on top, nesting it in the ice to steady it.

HOUSE "SOCO" BOURBON

Makes about 1 liter

I prefer to use dry ingredients to infuse liquor with other flavors because they have no moisture. This is especially true when it comes to fruit. The liquid in fresh fruit can make an infusion susceptible to quick spoilage. Dried fruit gives you all the flavor you want without any of the water that can shorten the shelf life of the final product. When making this infusion, we remove the cinnamon stick after 12 hours so that the spice doesn't overwhelm all the other flavors in the mixture.

1 liter 100-proof bonded bourbon

½ cup dried cherries

½ cup dried apricots

½ cup Dried Orange Wheels (page 74), cut in half before measuring

1 vanilla bean, split lengthwise in half

1 (3-inch) cinnamon stick

Combine the bourbon, cherries, apricots, orange slices, vanilla bean, and cinnamon stick in a 2-quart glass measuring cup or other container. (Reserve the empty bourbon bottle if you'd like to store the "SoCo" bourbon in it.)

Cover and let stand for 12 hours. Remove the cinnamon stick.

Re-cover the container and let stand for 12 to 24 hours.

Line a mesh strainer with cheesecloth and strain the infused bourbon through it into a clean container. Discard the fruit and vanilla bean. Transfer the "SoCo" bourbon to the reserved bottle or another container with a tight-fitting lid. Store in a cool place for up to 1 month. We always use it up in just a few days; beyond 1 month the flavor will begin to fade.

Amethyst Flip

Glassware 7.5-ounce cocktail coupe, chilled (see page 6)   **Serving ice** None

The sweet potato is so popular in the South that towns host annual festivals dedicated to the tuber, and princesses are crowned in its name. The state of North Carolina went so far as to declare it their state vegetable. But its American roots (no pun intended) long predate these contemporary tributes. In the sixteenth century, early Spanish explorers documented the presence of sweet potatoes in the areas now known as Louisiana, the Carolinas, and Mississippi. But its origins go back even further: the sweet potato was domesticated thousands of years ago in Central and South America.

Perhaps the reason behind our modern affinity for the sweet potato is that it was once a reliable staple food during times of scarcity. Dried sweet potato slices were even ground and brewed like coffee when lines of distribution of the real thing ran dry. Or perhaps it's the sweet potato's flavor, familiar but never boring. Whether baked, mashed, candied, fried, or folded into a pie crust, it reminds us

of family gatherings, abundance—even love. The sweet potato conveys warmth and nourishment and is often paired with aromatic spices that stir similar sentiments.

When pressing the juice from the sweet potato, the main problem is that the starch will ferment if it's not properly stabilized. From the beverage perspective, the most practical approach to stabilizing the starch is to make it into a syrup. This preparation gives us the confectionery note we're looking for and captures the purple sweet potato's beautiful color as a bonus. Trial and error led us to a classic flip style, which typically includes egg, spirits, sweetener, and some spice. Thus, we have transformed one of the South's favorite staples into an elegant, welcoming cocktail that showcases all of the region's best qualities.

continued

Amethyst Flip, continued

1 ounce cognac, such as Pierre Ferrand 1840

1 ounce sparkling wine

½ ounce sloe gin, such as Plymouth Sloe Gin

¾ ounce Sweet Potato Syrup (page 194)

¼ ounce Turbinado Syrup (page 192)

1 whole egg

GARNISH

Whole nutmeg

Pour the cognac, sparkling wine, sloe gin, Sweet Potato Syrup, Turbinado Syrup, and the egg into a cocktail shaker. Cover and dry shake vigorously 20 times. Open and fill the shaker with ice cubes. Cover and shake vigorously 40 times. Fine-strain into the chilled glass.

Garnish with a few grates of nutmeg.

Burnt Sugar

Glassware Rocks glass   **Serving ice** 1¼-inch cubes

I don't know if Burnt Sugar Cake is strictly Southern, but I do know for sure that it's all country. There's nothing like the flavor of this cake: it's almost like burnt sap, but in a good way, sweet and caramel-y and kind of weird. It's the sort of cake that conjures up thoughts of church potlucks and dinner at Grandma's house. The best way to know the flavor of the cake is to dig up a recipe on the internet and make one yourself. Or you can take my word for it that this cake was just begging to be honored with a delicious cocktail.

1 ounce reposado tequila, such as Tequila Ocho reposado

1 ounce Demerara rum, such as El Dorado 5-year

½ ounce burnt sugar syrup, such as Tippleman's

1 barspoon coffee liqueur

Fill the glass with ice cubes. Pour the tequila, rum, burnt sugar, and coffee liqueur into a mixing glass and fill with ice cubes. Stir 20 times with a barspoon. Strain into the rocks glass.

Landed Gentry

Glassware Rocks glass   **Serving ice** 1 Floral Ice Cube (recipe follows)

Alluding to the lavish lifestyle of the Antebellum South, the Landed Gentry looks and drinks elegant, with a bright, clear color and a beautiful mustard flower frozen inside a single large ice cube. Note that I use the term *landed gentry* with tongue planted firmly in cheek. The true landed gentry were a British class who could live entirely off the rental income generated by property their families owned. They weren't technically part of the aristocracy, but they were very well off. In Colonial America, especially in the South, plantation owners and other wealthy landholders (including many of the country's Founding Fathers) aspired to be gentry in their own right. But early Americans couldn't own vast property that had been handed down for generations: they hadn't been in the country long enough. And they couldn't live off rents paid to them, because even the grandest among the plantations were working farms run by their owners on the backs of slave labor. We now know that the Southern economy was wholly unsustainable. This emphasizes the contradiction inherent in imitating the trappings of a culture and class structure from which American colonists would soon—violently—declare themselves independent.

By the early nineteenth century, one symbol of wealth was ice, harvested from the surfaces of ponds and streams up north and transported to the South—indeed, all over the world. Some of the most coveted ice had flowers in it. To capture that natural spirit, we freeze tiny mustard flowers in the ice cube for this drink.

As for the spirits used in this cocktail, to symbolize the aspirations of those early American gentry (and of determined Americans everywhere), we use specific labels of French vermouth and bitters and Italian maraschino—all of which come from houses that were making these products in the nineteenth century. We round it out by using one of the finest tequilas: the Ocho Plata. It's the only tequila you should use in this drink to make the Landed Gentry well balanced and bold.

Absinthe mist
(see page 11) or
¼ ounce absinthe,
for the glass

1 ounce Tequila
Ocho Plata

½ ounce blanc
vermouth, such as
Dolin Blanc

½ ounce Suze bitters
aperitif

¼ ounce Luxardo
maraschino liqueur

1 barspoon agave
nectar

Mist the glass with the absinthe or pour
¼ ounce absinthe into it and turn to coat
the sides and bottom thoroughly. Place the
flower ice cube in the glass. Set aside.

Pour the tequila, vermouth, bitters,
maraschino, and agave into a mixing glass.
Stir 20 times with a barspoon. Strain into
the rocks glass.

FLORAL ICE CUBE

One of our local farmers provides us
with little sprays of the beautiful yellow
flowers that grow on his mustard plants.
The farmers' market is a good place to
find them. Alternatively, use another type
of edible flower—just make sure it was
grown to be eaten.

**Fresh mustard or
other edible flowers
(see Note)**

Have ready one or two 2-inch ice cube
trays. Soak the flowers in cool water
for 1 hour. Gently drain them. Cut each
mustard flower spray (and other flowers
as necessary) so it fits neatly into a single
cube opening. Place a spray or 1 or
2 flowers in each opening. Fill the tray
with water. Freeze solid.

Note The number of flowers you need
depends on how many ice cubes you're
making. For each cube, you'll need
1 mustard flower spray or 1 or 2 individual
flowers.

Attic Cellar Kalimocho

Glassware Rocks glass   **Serving Ice** 1¼-inch cubes

The Kalimotxo, spelled the Basque way (the *tx* makes a *ch* sound) and pronounced cal-ee-MO-cho, is said to have originated in the Basque country and is popular in Spain. It couldn't be simpler—equal parts red wine and cola served over ice—or more refreshing. Some call it the poor man's Sangria, which is probably why we thought of it when planning the Rural South menu. The Kalimotxo is a cocktail with no pretensions. Its straightforwardness appealed to us, as did the idea of a low-proof, wine-based cocktail. As we began to create our own version (using the phonetic spelling of Kalimocho for simplicity's sake), we started thinking about the part of the world it comes from and the kinds of wine that are made there—especially the fortified wines like Spanish sherry and Portuguese madeira.

People have been drinking madeira on what eventually became American soil since the first explorers arrived here. For centuries, madeira has been produced on a Portuguese archipelago about six hundred miles off the coast of mainland Portugal, which would have been a natural rest stop for ships traveling between Europe and the New World. Because the wine would spoil on those long voyages, madeira became a fortified wine. Adding a small amount of distilled alcohol increased its stability and guaranteed its status as one of the American colonies' most popular imports. Madeira had a huge presence in the Southern states throughout the nineteenth century, and George Washington, a native Virginian, was a dedicated fan.

Considering madeira's history in the South, it made sense to try it in our Kalimocho. We began to play around with a madeira made from Bual grapes, which has lots of fruit and spice. Adding both mezcal and ancho liqueur underscores the smoky notes, and the ancho gives it a bit of heat. When it all comes together in the glass, the resulting cocktail has a curiously enticing, musty quality appropriate for a menu inspired by the Rural South. I like to say that it drinks the way old books smell. It reminds me of climbing up into the attic or down into the cellar and opening a chest of long-forgotten keepsakes.

1 ounce madeira, such as Blandy's 5 Year Old Bual Madeira

¾ ounce mezcal

¼ ounce Ancho Reyes ancho chile liqueur

¼ ounce agave nectar

Topo Chico sparkling mineral water, for topping off

Pour the madeira, mezcal, liqueur, and agave into the glass. Stir with a barspoon a few times. Fill the glass with ice cubes. Stir a few more times. Top off with sparkling mineral water.

Farmhouse Gibson

Glassware 5.5-ounce cocktail coupe, chilled (see page 6)   **Serving ice** None

You may be surprised to find the Gibson in a book about Southern cocktails—in the Rural South chapter no less. The Gibson, which originated in San Francisco, is a classic gin martini with a pickled onion garnish. Pickling is an essential Southern tradition, for good reason. The ability to preserve food during the growing season—when vegetables, fruit, and meat are abundant—to be eaten during the winter was once key to survival. I love how a practice born of necessity resulted in a rich array of deliciousness and a custom of passing down treasured recipes from generation to generation. At dinner parties in the South, it's common to encounter a dish of something pickled: okra, peppers, tomatoes, cucumbers, onions, even pork. It seems that there's nothing a Southern cook can't pickle. So when I decided to include a Gibson on the menu, I knew just how to give it a Southern pedigree. I wanted the pickling brine to be an integral part of the cocktail, so I created a brine that would both make fabulous pickled onions and taste amazing with gin and vermouth. If you're reading this and find yourself dying for a Farmhouse Gibson *right now*, you're out of luck because you need to allow a little time for the pickling. I promise you it's worth the wait.

2 ounces London dry gin, such as Beefeater

1 ounce blanc vermouth, such as Dolin Blanc

2 barspoons sherry vinegar brine from Cocktail Onions (page 202)

2 dashes Regans' orange bitters

GARNISH

1 Cocktail Onion (page 202)

Pour the gin, vermouth, vinegar brine, and orange bitters into a mixing glass. Fill the glass with ice cubes and stir 20 times with a barspoon. Strain into the chilled glass.

To garnish, thread the onion on a cocktail pick and lay across the rim of the glass.

Rose Boulevard

Glassware 5.5-ounce cocktail coupe, chilled (see page 6)   **Serving ice** None

I love the smell of roses, especially dried roses, which have a different scent than fresh ones. Fresh roses have a vibrant, citrusy, "green" smell, while dried ones are more intense. There's an almost confectionary quality to their aroma—like a potpourri, with its combination of cinnamon, bark, and dusty undertones. We wanted to capture that essence in a cocktail but knew we couldn't rely on rose water, which is much closer to fresh roses. After playing around a bit, we discovered that infusing bourbon with dried roses created exactly the dustiness we wanted. With that, we moved in the direction of the classic Boulevardier—whiskey, sweet vermouth, and Campari—with its rich, bittersweet flavor. For the Rose Boulevard, we swap out the sweet vermouth and Campari for Aperol Aperitivo and Cocchi Americano Rosa, which contribute bright, floral, citrusy notes along with the deeper flavors of roots, berries, and spices.

1 ounce Rose-Infused Bourbon (recipe follows)

1 ounce Aperol Aperitivo liqueur

¾ ounce Cocchi Americano Rosa

Pour the bourbon, Aperol, and Cocchi Rosa into a mixing glass. Fill the glass with ice cubes. Stir 20 times with a barspoon. Strain into the chilled glass.

ROSE-INFUSED BOURBON

Makes 1 liter

Dried rosebuds and petals are available online. Make sure that you use roses that are explicitly marked as being food safe.

1 liter 80-proof bourbon

1 ounce food-grade dried rosebuds and petals

Combine the bourbon and rosebuds and petals in a 2-quart glass measuring cup or other container. (Reserve the empty bourbon bottle if you'd like to store the infused bourbon in it.) Cover and let stand for 1 hour.

Line a mesh strainer set over a bowl with cheesecloth. Strain the bourbon through the cheesecloth. Discard the rosebuds and petals. Transfer the infused bourbon to the reserved bottle or another container with a tight-fitting lid. Store in a cool place for up to 1 month; after this time, the rose flavor will begin to fade.

The Saltwater South

After focusing on small cities in the Rural South menu, we moved to the coasts and the booming Saltwater South. This menu incorporates ingredients found in and around Southern port cities and coastal regions, such as Charleston, New Orleans, Galveston, and Savannah, as well as spirits and wine with coastal terroir from all over the world. It's impossible to overstate the role of ports in creating vibrant communities. They were synonymous with progress, enabling trade and movement of products all over the world. Two hundred years ago, if you lived in an American city, by definition you lived in a port; there wasn't any other kind of city. Being close to or living in a port city meant that you weren't isolated. And before roads and railroads, the communities that grew fastest—those that employed people, supported commerce, and so on—either had a port or were close to one. These cities had the easiest access to many of the resources that are represented on this menu, including spirits from Europe and rum from the Caribbean. Props go to the Southern Foodways Alliance (see page 205) for coining the term *Saltwater South*. When I first heard it on their podcast, *Gravy*, I knew I'd adopt it as the title of this menu and chapter. It encapsulates the concept I wanted to showcase. We're not talking about just a single region here; we're talking about an entire way of life.

While I wanted to highlight this fascinating story, I worried that the concept was hard to express without a lot of explanation. We needed to *show* it rather than *tell* it. So we went all in: changing the whole cocktail menu as well as the food, introducing many seafood-based snacks, as well as a beer-and-wine program highlighting those from coastal regions. Every one of them included ingredients with saltwater roots and came with a great story. Launching this menu during the height of summer was intentional; the ingredients we wanted to highlight lend themselves to the kinds of things we want to consume when the mercury is rising. Seasonality is a factor in cocktail development just as it is with food. It goes beyond the obvious—for example, I wouldn't have a hot drink like the Tequila Toddy (page 60) on the menu in August. And while seasonality influences the culinary ingredients we use (I can make the Vinegar & Rye [page 105] only when figs are in season, for example), there's more to it than that. Seasonality greatly influences the spirits used and how they are combined in a cocktail. When it's 110 degrees outside, you need to give people a reason to go out rather than to just stay home. The cocktails need to "drink cool." So we give them higher minerality and acidity from ingredients such as sherry and verjus. Summer cocktails are tart, sweet, and sometimes contain a touch of salinity. There's an interesting parallel between what the ports meant to the South and what this menu meant to us. Just as the ports facilitated greater commerce, this menu allowed us to go outside the common wheelhouse of Southern spirits, such as bourbon, and use many more coastal spirits to introduce light and tart components into these refreshing summer drinks.

Preservationist

Barware Collins glass + straw   **Serving ice** Crushed

It's difficult to find an ingredient more tied to the Saltwater South than, well, salt. For thousands of years, people have used salt to preserve food, which of course every civilization needs to survive.

From the beginning of recorded history, humans have linked their fortunes to salt. In fact, the word *salary* comes from the Latin word for salt. We wanted a cocktail on the menu that would symbolize this, and the Preservationist became that cocktail, based on fresh lemon juice and a house-made salt tincture.

GARNISH

Himalayan pink or kosher salt

1 lemon wedge, for rubbing the rim

1 lemon wheel

1½ ounces Mellow Corn whiskey

¾ ounce dry vermouth, such as Dolin dry

¾ ounce freshly squeezed lemon juice

½ ounce Turbinado Syrup (page 192)

6 dashes Salt Tincture (page 198)

To prepare the glass, pour the salt for the garnish in a saucer or small, shallow plate. Rub the outer rim of the glass with the lemon wedge. Roll the top of the glass in the salt to fully coat the outer rim. Fill the glass with crushed ice and set aside with the lemon wheel.

Pour the whiskey, vermouth, lemon juice, syrup, and tincture into a cocktail shaker. Fill the shaker with ice cubes. Cover and shake vigorously 20 times. Strain into the glass. Place the straw in the glass.

Garnish with the lemon wheel.

Low Country

Barware 8-ounce brandy snifter + straw   **Serving ice** Crushed

According to lore, South Carolina's low country became the birthplace of America's rice production in 1685, when the captain of a hobbled ship out of Madagascar docked in Charleston for repairs and presented a local settler with a bag of seed. The mythology lives on one hundred years later. When Thomas Jefferson was the U.S. ambassador to France in the late 1780s, he purportedly smuggled a few grains of arborio-like Italian rice out of Europe. Those seeds made their way to low-country farmers so that they could add variety to their signature crop. For the next hundred years or more, the heat, moisture, and slave labor made Carolina low country the main producer of America's rice. Sometime around the Civil War, production moved farther south to Louisiana and beyond, and as far west as California. Today, growers such as Glenn Roberts at Anson Mills are bringing true Carolina Gold rice back to its roots. We like to think we're doing our part for the cause with this cocktail. We blend house-made rice cream with cachaça, a cane sugar–based spirit, to produce a tropical, piña colada–like drink.

1½ ounces cachaça, such as Novo Fogo

2 ounces Rice Cream (recipe follows)

½ ounce freshly squeezed lime juice

¼ ounce absinthe, preferably Kübler

¼ ounce Turbinado Syrup (page 192)

GARNISH

Cinnamon stick

Fill the glass with crushed ice. Pour the cachaça, Rice Cream, lime juice, absinthe, and syrup into a cocktail shaker. Fill the shaker with ice cubes. Close and shake vigorously 20 times. Strain into the snifter. Place the straw in the glass.

Garnish with a few grates of cinnamon.

continued

RICE CREAM

Makes about 2 cups (16 ounces)

Before it was possible to find really good commercially produced orgeat, I made my own by soaking almonds in water and then simmering the strained liquid with sugar to make syrup. That process inspired me to make rice cream. It's based on an infusion of water and flavorful rice, such as Carolina Gold from Anson Mills (see Resources, page 205), which is combined with sugar, cream, and condensed milk.

1 cup Carolina Gold rice or other medium-grain white rice

2 cups water

¼ cup granulated sugar

2 tablespoons whipping cream

2 tablespoons condensed milk

½ ounce cachaça

Pulverize the rice in a food processor as finely as possible. Transfer to a bowl. Add the water. Let stand for 24 hours.

Strain through a cheesecloth-lined mesh sieve into a glass measuring cup; discard the rice.

Pour 1½ cups of the rice water into a saucepan (discard the rest). Stir in the sugar, cream, and condensed milk. Bring to a low simmer over low heat. Simmer gently, stirring occasionally, for 15 minutes.

Remove from the heat and let cool. Stir in the cachaça. Transfer to a covered container and store in the refrigerator for up to 3 days. Shake before using.

Hot July Moon

Barware 5.5-ounce cordial glass or champagne flute   **Serving ice** None

This cocktail was based on a Pisco Sour, made with pisco (a spirit made from grapes in coastal regions of Peru and Chile), citrus, syrup, and an egg white. Adding strawberry puree and rosé wine to the formula gave us a beautifully balanced cocktail that tasted fruity and tart. One of our bartenders said the cocktail reminded him of "strawberry wine." Instantly, the term brought me back about two decades when the song "Strawberry Wine," by country singer Deana Carter, was in regular rotation on the radio. It's an uncannily catchy ballad about how falling in love for the first time under a "hot July moon" is bittersweet "like strawberry wine." It's the kind of song that puts you in a pleasant state of mind—just as this cocktail does.

¾ ounce Peruvian pisco, such as Machu Pisco

¾ ounce rosé wine

¾ ounce Strawberry Puree (recipe follows)

½ ounce Turbinado Syrup (page 192)

½ ounce freshly squeezed lime juice

1 egg white

GARNISH

1 strawberry

Pour the pisco, wine, strawberry puree, syrup, lime juice, and egg white into a cocktail shaker. Cover and shake vigorously 20 times. Open the shaker and fill it with ice cubes. Cover and shake vigorously 40 times. Fine-strain into the glass.

To garnish, make a slice in the base of the strawberry and place it on the rim of the glass.

STRAWBERRY PUREE

Makes about 1½ cups (12 ounces)

Strawberries will generally be very sweet at the height of their season. If the berries you use are a little tart, you may add another 1 to 2 tablespoons of sugar.

1 pint fresh strawberries, hulled

½ cup sugar, plus more as needed

½ ounce neutral grain spirit or vodka

Place the strawberries in a blender and process until pureed. Transfer the puree to a saucepan and stir in the sugar.

Simmer over very low heat, stirring frequently, until the sugar is dissolved, about 20 minutes. Remove from the heat and let cool completely.

Stir in the grain spirit or vodka.

Store in a covered container in the refrigerator for up to 1 week. Shake before using.

Vinegar & Rye

Barware Rocks glass + straw   **Serving ice** Crushed

I don't know whether it's our history or our natural temperament, but Southerners are partial to managing expectations. I didn't want to sneak up on anyone, so I opted for full disclosure in this cocktail's name (though it's just a barspoonful of vinegar). This is one of the best vinegars you'll ever taste—made from Banyuls sweet wine and aged in oak barrels. It contributes depth and kicks in just the zing you want at the end of a sip of this drink, built on the mellow marriage of rye and rainwater madeira with sweet fresh figs. If I had my wish, I could get luscious, ripe figs all year long so that we could always serve the Vinegar & Rye. It's *that* good.

1 whole fig, trimmed and halved

1 ounce 100-proof bonded rye whiskey

1 ounce rainwater madeira

½ ounce Turbinado Syrup (page 192)

1 barspoon freshly squeezed lime juice

1 barspoon Banyuls vinegar

GARNISH

2 mint sprigs

½ fresh fig

Place both halves of the fig into a cocktail shaker. Muddle until pulverized. Add the rye, madeira, syrup, lime juice, and vinegar. Fill the shaker with ice cubes. Shake vigorously 40 times. Pour into the glass. Fill the glass to the rim with crushed ice. Place the straw in the glass.

To garnish, press the mint sprigs between your fingers to release their aroma and tuck them into the ice. Lay the fig half, cut side up, on the ice or tuck it stem side down into the ice next to the mint.

Truth & Slant

Barware Rocks glass   **Serving ice** 1 (2-inch) cube

"Tell all the Truth but tell it slant," opens Emily Dickinson's 1868 poem, an elegant ode to the value of occasionally wrapping veracity in a veil of obfuscation. She might as well have had booze in mind when she wrote those words. Dickinson was probably thinking about something else, but the history of alcohol boils down to telling stories about all the ways people have become intoxicated for millennia, and it's hard to find less reliable storytellers than drunk people. Which leads us to this unique combination of ingredients—unlike any other cocktail we've made—that delivers unexpectedly delicious results. A few items in particular make it work: The Famous Grouse Smoky Black (formerly The Black Grouse) scotch has just the right degree of smokiness; the Acqua di Cedro lemon liqueur brings in texture and a distinct type of lemon flavor; and the rainwater madeira adds acidity to the cocktail without putting any juice into it. The result is a boozy sipper, slightly on the sweet side, with a nice acidity and lemon fruit flavor, which drinks almost like a low-alcohol wine. It's a cocktail that presents one way but turns out to be concealing part of the story. Here, truth and slant are intertwined and served on the rocks.

1 ounce The Famous Grouse Smoky Black scotch

1 ounce rainwater madeira

¾ ounce Nardini Acqua di Cedro lemon liqueur

2 dashes Scrappy's Chocolate Bitters

Place the ice cube in the glass. Pour the scotch, madeira, lemon liqueur, and bitters into a mixing glass. Fill the glass with ice cubes. Stir 20 times with a barspoon. Strain into the rocks glass.

Eudora

Barware Collins glass   **Serving ice** 1¼-inch cubes

This cocktail originated at the Women at Work Symposium held by the Southern Foodways Alliance in 2013. It was created for one of the weekend's main events, a Lincoln-Douglas–style debate between food journalists Kim Severson and Kat Kinsman to determine which is more quintessentially Southern: cake or pie. The worthiness of the question is indisputable, and the debate was one of the most spirited I've seen. But for me the biggest challenge was being tasked with providing the audience with a cocktail that could accompany both. When creating a cocktail to pair with food, you must consider what's going to be on the drinker's palate before they take a sip—in this case, cake and pie. The difficulty of pairing cocktails with sweet foods is that you can't rely on sugar to provide balance in the drink; instead, the focus is on the overall balance between cocktail and food. This mission called for something tasty yet unobtrusive, and above all it needed to have some acidity. Talking with Southern Foodways Alliance Director John T. Edge about my concept for this cocktail, I suggested using celery juice. With all that sweetness up front, it needed something savory and "long"—an element that would elongate the flavors and rinse the palate. John T. mentioned that celery soda was a favorite of Eudora Welty, one of the twentieth century's most celebrated Southern writers. With that, I had both the flavor I wanted to highlight *and* the perfect name for the cocktail. Celery marries beautifully with gin and manzanilla, a variety of fino sherry produced near the port town of Sanlúcar de Barrameda on the southwest coast of Spain. Sherry is extremely food friendly, so it was a natural fit with both the savory celery in the cocktail and the cake and pie it would accompany.

2 ounces manzanilla sherry

½ ounce London dry gin

1 ounce pressed celery juice

¼ ounce Turbinado Syrup (page 192)

1 barspoon freshly squeezed lemon juice

Topo Chico sparkling mineral water, for topping off

GARNISH

1 stalk celery

Fill the glass with ice cubes. Pour the sherry, gin, celery juice, syrup, and lemon juice into a cocktail shaker. Fill the shaker with ice cubes. Shake vigorously 20 times. Strain into the glass. Top off with sparkling mineral water.

Use a vegetable peeler to peel off a 4-inch-long ribbon (see Note, page 149) of celery. Garnish with the celery ribbon.

Cape Fear Cooler

Barware Rocks glass   **Serving ice** 1¼-inch cubes

This fizzy cooler is named for the lush coastal plain around Wilmington, North Carolina, where many Scots began to settle in the mid-eighteenth century. We wanted to honor those early waves of rugged Scotsmen who moved from one seaside area to another, an ocean away. Since the native spirit of Scotland is scotch, we used Laphroaig 10-year-old single malt from the island of Islay. Scotch made on this island is a prime example of coastal spirits, which often have an element of salinity. Laphroaig also has a distinct peaty smokiness. In this cocktail, the scotch's particular elements are blended with pureed watermelon and topped off with carbonated *verjus*, or "green juice." *Verjus* is made from the pressed, unripened grapes that would normally be used for wine production but didn't make the cut. My friend Andrew Paul Mariani at Scribe Winery in Sonoma used pinot noir estate grapes (the same ones used for the winery's most coveted wines) to create a *verjus* just for us. In this cocktail, the *verjus* is carbonated for a lovely effect (you'll need a soda siphon [see page 2]). The resulting drink combines deep undertones with a bright, subtly sweet effervescence.

1 ounce Laphroaig 10-year-old scotch

1 ounce Watermelon Puree (recipe follows)

1½ ounces carbonated verjus, preferably made with pinot noir grapes

GARNISH

1 watermelon wedge

Pour the scotch and watermelon puree in the glass and stir lightly. Fill the glass with ice cubes. Top off with the carbonated verjus and stir gently. Garnish with the watermelon wedge.

WATERMELON PUREE

Makes about 1½ cups (12 ounces)

This watermelon puree balances out the tart, smoky elements in the Cape Fear Cooler.

2 cups 1-inch cubes seedless watermelon

1 cup granulated sugar

1 ounce vodka

Place the watermelon, sugar, and vodka in a blender and puree until smooth. Strain the puree through a fine-mesh strainer. Transfer to a covered container and refrigerate until cold before using. Store in the refrigerator for up to 3 days.

Saratoga

Barware 5.5-ounce cocktail coupe, chilled (see page 6)   **Serving ice** None

If you're a cocktail aficionado, your eyebrow no doubt arched when you saw this classic cocktail tucked here in the Saltwater South. But even if you consider yourself a purist, I'm sure you'll appreciate my reasoning. (If not, I'm certain that you'll appreciate the cocktail itself.) The Saratoga comports to the straightforward "equal parts" genre of cocktails, using equal portions of three liquors—in this case rye, cognac, and sweet vermouth. This simple concept is surprisingly easy to get wrong, most often by using a sweet vermouth that plays discordant notes with the rye and cognac. A better choice is the sweet vermouth made by Vermuts Miró, a coastal winery in the Catalonia region of northeastern Spain. It is herbal and dry with a good dose of salinity, which are imparted to the cocktail—all the reasons this Saratoga needs to be an honorary member of the Saltwater South.

¾ ounce 100-proof bonded rye whiskey

¾ ounce cognac, preferably Pierre Ferrand 1840

¾ ounce Miró Rojo sweet vermouth

1 barspoon Turbinado Syrup (page 192)

2 dashes Angostura bitters

GARNISH

1 thyme sprig

Pour the rye, cognac, vermouth, syrup, and bitters into a mixing glass. Fill the glass with ice cubes. Stir 20 times with a barspoon. Strain into the chilled glass.

To garnish, lay the thyme sprig across the rim of the glass.

Orchard Spritz

Glassware Standard white wine glass   **Serving ice** 1¼-inch cubes

Although we invented the summery, light Orchard Spritz a full year after we introduced the Saltwater South menu, we knew that its salinity and tartness made it right at home. The Urbitarte cider is the key component here. Its acidity and complex, musty flavors really make this something special. Note that Urbitarte is flat, so we top it off with a little soda.

1 ounce Herb-Infused Rue Grappa (recipe follows)	2 ounces flat, dry, Basque-style cider, preferably Urbitarte
1 ounce freshly squeezed lime juice	Soda water
¾ ounce orgeat	**GARNISH**
¼ ounce Simple Syrup (page 193)	Rosemary sprig
	Castelvetrano olive

Fill the glass with ice. Pour the grappa, lime juice, orgeat, and syrup into a cocktail shaker. Fill the shaker with ice cubes. Cover and shake vigorously 20 times.

Strain into the glass. Add the cider and top off with soda. Gently stir with a barspoon.

To garnish, press the rosemary sprig between your fingers to release its aroma and place it in the glass. Thread the olive on a cocktail pick and lay it across the rim of the glass.

HERB-INFUSED RUE GRAPPA

Makes 1 liter

Grappa is an Italian pomace brandy, meaning it is produced using the leftovers from wine making after the grapes are crushed.

1 liter rue grappa, such as Candolini Ruta Grappa	1 ounce rosemary sprigs
	1 ounce thyme sprigs
1 ounce oregano sprigs	

Combine the grappa and the oregano, rosemary, and thyme sprigs in a 2-quart glass measuring cup or other container. (Reserve the empty grappa bottle if you'd like to store the infused grappa in it.) Cover and let stand overnight or up to 12 hours.

Line a mesh strainer set over a bowl with cheesecloth. Strain the grappa through the cheesecloth. Use a wooden spoon to press on the herbs to extract as much liquid as possible from them. Discard the herbs. Set the strainer over another bowl and strain the grappa through the cheesecloth once more to remove any remaining bits of herbs and oils (if left in the grappa they will create a haze in the infused spirit). Transfer the grappa to the reserved bottle or another container with a tight-fitting lid. Store in a cool place for up to 1 month; the flavors will begin to fade after that.

Trading with the Enemy

In the fall of 2015, we concluded our cycle of stories of the South with a menu rooted in the Southern experience of the Civil War. I had intended to end these historically inspired menus this way, because the cooler time of year seemed like the best time to reflect on the strong emotions that come with examining North-South relationships. Talking about the war is an integral part of understanding what is Southern and what is not. But the subject is difficult, and I wanted to find a way to talk about these topics. Among the most interesting aspects of the war is the huge amount of trade that went on across the battle lines. Throughout the war, munitions, spirits, salt, and especially cotton were traded actively (if somewhat illicitly). The versatility of cotton made it more coveted than wool. The South had the plantations but the North had the mills, and they absolutely needed each other to manufacture and export products. Once the two sides were at war little to no formal cooperation took place between them, but unofficially off-the-books commerce flourished.

These Civil War "trading-with-the-enemy" stories underscore the ongoing interdependence of North and South (but not the real and profound misery of the war). So I created a menu informed by the regions and ingredients integral to the trade between the enemies, and by the ways people on both sides of the Mason-Dixon line managed to survive. The tales of the characters in this chapter resonate powerfully. There's the general who held the Union advance at bay with a ruse. There's Champagne Charlie (see page 122), who came to the United States as the war got underway just to seek payment for his champagne and wound up in jail and penniless. There had to be a cocktail named Borrowed Time (page 126) on this menu, for this was a group of people living on just that.

Butternut Effort

Barware Rocks glass   **Serving ice** 1¼-inch cubes

In the late 1700s, the U.S. military began supplying troops with two-to-four-ounce rations of rum or whiskey (the amount changed several times over the years). The practice of rationing spirits ended in 1832, replaced by rations of coffee and sugar—presumably to foster a more sober and alert (if less cheerful) fighting force. A few decades later, during occasional breaks in the fighting early in the Civil War, Union and Confederate soldiers would meet and trade Northern coffee for Southern whiskey and tobacco. Periodic displays of camaraderie aside, the Northerners called their Confederate counterparts "butternuts"—probably for the light brown color of their uniforms. (This might have resulted from fading of the original gray or being dyed with butternut tree bark and shells.)

The mutual reliance and the characters of both camps inspired this cocktail, which features a strong coffee flavor with complementary tart notes.

1 ounce dry red wine, such as a Rioja

1 ounce Demerara rum, such as El Dorado 5-year

1 ounce coffee liqueur, such as Heering Coffee Liqueur

½ ounce freshly squeezed lime juice

Fill the glass with ice cubes. Pour the wine, rum, liqueur, and lime juice into a cocktail shaker. Fill the shaker with ice cubes. Cover and shake vigorously 20 times. Strain the cocktail over the ice into the glass.

Trick of the Trade

Barware 7.5-ounce cocktail coupe, chilled (see page 6)   **Serving ice** None

Among the many stories of trading with the enemy during the Civil War, the version about one particular shipman may be the most retold of them all: he traded *himself*. Every time he and his crew (more like pirates) were captured, they'd switch flags to the side of whoever had caught them, as long as the price was right. When they finally found themselves cornered on their ship, they still refused to go quietly. He and his men stalled the lawful apprehension for a few days by covering themselves with flour. The sight of them walking around with white faces discouraged their would-be captors from boarding the ship—they were convinced they were suffering from some highly infectious disease. I can't vouch for the details of this yarn, but the first time I heard it, visions of ghostly cocktails like this one sprang to mind.

1½ ounces 100-proof bonded bourbon

1 ounce cream sherry, such as Hidalgo

½ ounce Rancio Sec wine

1 barspoon Turbinado Syrup (page 192)

Pour the bourbon, sherry, wine, and syrup into a mixing glass. Fill the glass with ice cubes. Stir 20 times with a barspoon. Strain into the chilled glass.

The Ruse

Barware 13.5-ounce zombie glass + straw　　**Serving ice** Crushed

One of most unbelievable Civil War stories I've heard is about a general based out of Galveston who (single-handedly or with a small handful of soldiers, depending on who's telling the story) held off the Union navy for days (or weeks or months, depending on who's telling the story) with a ruse. He painted a bunch of logs black and set them up—along with the one real cannon he possessed—aimed at the bay. Whenever he saw the enemy approaching, he'd set off his cannon and then hoot and holler and generally make an enormous commotion. The enemy ships would leave, convinced that he had serious artillery and manpower when all he had was a bunch of logs. It's said that when the Union soldiers finally caught him, they couldn't believe that one solitary guy had thwarted them for so long. Versions of this story have been told forever, and I can't say for sure whether it was one guy and ten logs or ten guys and one log— but the idea inspired a great name for this cocktail. At Julep we use only one kind of sherry for The Ruse—*Palo Cortado*, which translates to "cut logs."

1 ounce Palo Cortado sherry

¾ ounce 80-proof bourbon

¾ ounce amaro, such as Averna

¾ ounce freshly squeezed lemon juice

½ ounce orgeat

½ ounce Turbinado Syrup (page 192)

1 dash Regans' orange bitters, for topping off

GARNISH

Half an orange wheel

1 mint leaf

Pour the sherry, bourbon, amaro, lemon juice, orgeat, syrup, and bitters in the glass. Fill the glass three-quarters full with crushed ice. Stir with a barspoon until the outside of the glass is frosted. Fill the glass with crushed ice. Place the straw in the glass.

To garnish, shape the half orange wheel into a nest and skewer it with a cocktail pick and place on the glass rim. Press the mint leaf between your fingers to release its aroma and tuck it in the orange wheel nest. Place the garnish on top of the ice.

Liquid Currency

Barware 7.5-ounce cocktail coupe, chilled (see page 6)   **Serving ice** None

Charles Camille Heidsieck, or "Champagne Charlie," was a nineteenth-century champagne merchant from Reims, France. He traveled to the United States in 1852 and, realizing the huge potential of the American market, set himself up with an agent in New York. So successful was his export business that by the early 1860s a huge portion of his assets were tied up in America. As soon as the war broke out, he set sail for the United States seeking payment from his agent, who, unfortunately, declined to repay Heidsieck, using as flimsy justification the recently enacted federal law absolving all U.S. debtors of their debts. (Never mind that the law was designed to dry up funds to the Confederacy and had nothing to do with paying for French wine.) Champagne Charlie was left with no choice but to set out for New Orleans and try to recoup some of his money from the merchants. What he found there was a city in bankruptcy. One merchant, having no currency to repay him, gave him a large quantity of highly valuable cotton in lieu of cash. Heidsieck's attempts to smuggle it out through the port at Mobile, Alabama, were foiled when the Union sank the ships that had been stowing the cotton for shipment to France. In the meantime, all routes to the North had been blocked. The French consulate in Mobile gave him a diplomatic pouch for the consulate in New Orleans, to ensure

his safe passage to the city and back to France. But upon arrival, he found the city in the hands of the Union—as he soon found himself. The pouch was seized and found to be holding official documents from a French textile firm regarding Confederate uniforms. Heidsieck was charged with espionage and imprisoned, prompting an international diplomatic incident that would eventually involve Napoleon III and Abraham Lincoln. The Heidsieck Incident, as it became known, ended when a penniless Champagne Charlie was finally released and allowed to return to Reims.

If the saga had ended there, Heidsieck producers and the Heidsieck Incident would have been no more than colorful footnotes in the stories of champagne and the Civil War. Luckily, the brother of Charles's former agent—who by some accounts also owed Heidsieck money—settled the unpaid debts by giving over the land deeds to a large portion of a tiny town in the American West called Denver. Selling off those parcels for a tidy sum likely played a large role in saving the label. Today Piper-Heidsieck is one of the largest premier Champagne houses in France, and the Heidsieck Incident is another episode in the liquid history of the Civil War.

1½ ounces
sparkling wine

½ ounce 100-proof
bonded rye whiskey

½ ounce amaro,
preferably Zucca

¼ ounce Combier
rose liqueur

½ ounce freshly
squeezed lemon juice

¼ ounce Simple
Syrup (page 193)

1 egg white

GARNISH

Angostura mist (see
page 11) or 3 dashes
Angostura bitters

Pour the sparkling wine, rye, amaro,
rose liqueur, lemon juice, syrup, and egg
white into a cocktail shaker. Cover and
dry shake vigorously 20 times. Open and
fill the shaker with ice cubes. Cover and
shake vigorously 40 times. Fine-strain into
the chilled glass. To garnish, spray the
Angostura mist once over the surface of
the cocktail or add 3 dashes of bitters.

Borrowed Time

Barware Standard white wine glass   **Serving ice** 1 (1¼-inch) cube

During the war, Northern textile merchants and the Union army provided the South with manufactured goods, artillery, and medicine in exchange for cotton. It was a mutually beneficial—if unorthodox—trading relationship. With raw materials but no manufacturing, the South needed these items to sustain its war effort. At the same time, cotton was displacing wool as the world's most popular fabric. So the Union—that is, the United States—facilitated these trades to sustain its overall export economy. Hence, an underground trading system developed to facilitate the exchange of these goods through the hands of merchants. Borrowed Time is a nod to the smoke and mirrors of economic treason that went on with the collusion of both sides.

1 ounce Laird's Jersey Lightning Apple Brandy, plus ¼ ounce for burning the juniper berries

1 ounce filtered water

¾ ounce Carpano Bianco vermouth

½ ounce Domaine de Canton ginger liqueur

2 or 3 fresh pine needles, broken up

3 juniper berries

GARNISH

2 or 3 fresh pine needles

Pour 1 ounce of apple brandy and the water, vermouth, and ginger liqueur into a mixing glass. Set aside.

Place the broken pine needle on a saucer. Put the juniper berries on top of the needles and carefully pour the remaining ¼ ounce of apple brandy directly on top of the berries. Use a kitchen torch or lighter to ignite the brandy, and smoke the berries until they are lightly burning. Immediately place the wine glass upside down over the berries so the smoke fills the glass.

Turn the glass over and immediately pour in the contents of the mixing glass.

To garnish, place the burned berries in the glass (discarding the burned pine needles) and place 2 or 3 fresh pine needles in the glass. Place the ice cube in the glass.

Morning Call

Barware Collins glass   **Serving ice** 1¼-inch cubes

Before the Civil War, Matamoros, across the Rio Grande from Brownsville, Texas, was a small and quiet Mexican town. But that changed during the war. Matamoros's proximity to open waters and its location outside the United States—out of reach of the Union blockade—rendered it a crucial port as well as the hub of a vibrant black market. But the border town's benefits were not enjoyed by Texas alone. Writing to Union general Lew Wallace in 1865, a correspondent reported that "Matamoros is to the rebellion west of the Mississippi what New York is to the United States—its great commercial and financial center, feeding and clothing the rebellion, arming and equipping, furnishing it materials of war and a specie basis of circulation that has almost displaced Confederate paper. . . . The entire Confederate Government is greatly sustained by resources from this port." Such an enormous number of English-speaking speculators came to Matamoros that an English-language daily newspaper, *Morning Call,* sprang up. The paper was short-lived, however, for soon after the war ended, Matamoros returned to being simply a quiet town on the border.

1½ ounces Tequila Ocho blanco

2 barspoons mezcal

½ ounce agave nectar

½ ounce freshly squeezed lime juice

Hibiscus-Infused Tonic (recipe follows), for topping off

GARNISH

1 fresh hibiscus flower

1 lime wedge

Fill the glass with ice cubes. Pour the tequila, mezcal, agave, and lime juice into a cocktail shaker. Fill the shaker with ice cubes and shake vigorously 20 times. Strain into the glass. Top off with the tonic.

To garnish, push a cocktail pick through the hibiscus flower and lime wedge and place on the glass rim.

continued

HIBISCUS-INFUSED TONIC

Makes 1 liter

In Spain, I drank a hibiscus tonic for the first time. It's commercially produced there but not distributed in the United States. So when I returned home, I created my own hibiscus tonic.

½ cup dried hibiscus flowers

2 (½-liter) bottles tonic water, such as Fever Tree

Place the hibiscus flowers in a bowl or a 2-liter glass measuring cup. Pour the tonic over the flowers. Cover loosely and let stand for 20 minutes. Strain the tonic through a fine mesh strainer, or a mesh strainer lined with cheesecloth, into a 1-liter soda siphon. Reserve the flowers for the garnish. Close the siphon and load it with a CO_2 cartridge. Shake the siphon several times to charge.

Appalachian Whip

Barware Copper tumbler or other 10-ounce glass + straw   **Serving ice** Crushed

During the Civil War, the Appalachian Mountain range was particularly volatile, with cities like Knoxville, Tennessee, changing hands multiple times. William "Parson" Brownlow, a preacher and publisher of the *Knoxville Whig* (and later, governor of Tennessee) was an anti-secessionist who refused to pledge loyalty to the Confederate States. Knowing the authorities were after him, he fled south to a Union stronghold in South Carolina. Eventually he was arrested for treason, and during his incarceration, he leaked his journal entries recounting the poor treatment of Union prisoners in Confederate jails. He was turned over to the Union, whereupon he whipped up audiences across Northern Appalachia on a speaking tour that stretched through New York, Pennsylvania, Ohio, and West Virginia. Parson Brownlow was the original Appalachian Whip.

10 mint leaves

1½ ounces 100-proof bonded rye whiskey

½ ounce Pedro Ximénez sherry, such as El Candado

½ ounce Crème Giffard Pêche de Vigne liqueur

½ ounce freshly squeezed lemon juice

¼ ounce Turbinado Syrup (page 192)

Ginger beer, for topping off

GARNISH

1 long swath orange zest

8 to 10 whole cloves

Fill the glass with crushed ice. Place the mint leaves in a cocktail shaker. Pour in the rye, sherry, pêche (peach) liqueur, lemon juice, and syrup. Fill the shaker with ice cubes. Close and shake vigorously 40 times. Fine-strain the cocktail into the glass. Top off with the ginger beer. Place the straw in the glass.

To garnish, shape the orange zest into a nest and skewer it with a cocktail pick. Tuck the cloves into the nest and place it on top of the ice.

Mostly Southern Classics

A persistent question for anyone who cares deeply about cocktail culture is, "What makes a cocktail a classic?" And what defines a Southern classic? In general, classics are cocktails that have provenance; that is, a particular person created them in a specific place. And Southern classics are further demarcated by the regions they come from. On the most basic level, these cocktails are the staples in the South. They provide an anchor, a reassuring familiarity. You can't be a Southern bar without a Sazerac, for example. For practical purposes, these established drinks are worthy enough to be popular selections on menus across the country—South or North, inland or coast. (Note that this chapter is called "Mostly" Southern Classics because it includes a few cocktails that didn't originate in the South but are nonetheless celebrated here.)

Still, one might wonder why we hold on to these traditions with so many new cocktails being created by ambitious mixologists every day. The reason is that acknowledging the importance of these drinks enables Southern culture to endure.

We can't talk about Southern drinking without talking about the Southern drinks that most people know. These are not the only cocktails I learned to make first, but they validate everything I've done. They are on our menus and in this book to provide a frame of reference. There's an adage that you can't invent anything new until you know the fundamentals. Although I took a nontraditional path, my experience proves the rule. Without these classics Julep would be just another bar, and I'd be just another bartender slinging drinks. It's similar to how many of us are raised with little knowledge of our ancestry, and we seek out the stories when we're grown. The cocktails that follow exemplify the rules demonstrated in every other cocktail in this book and in every cocktail we serve at Julep—even those that break all the rules. By sharing this curated selection, I want to show that the cocktails I invent come from a place and a tradition. My cocktails are intentional. These classics are my roots and the roots of the bar. And after all, if the Southern classics didn't exist, Julep wouldn't have so many rich stories to tell.

Crescent City

Barware 5.5-ounce cocktail coupe, chilled (see page 6)   **Serving ice** None

The recipe for a drink called the Fluffy Ruffles, made from sweet vermouth, rum, and lime rind, was published in 1916. Apparently the Fluffy Ruffles was adapted to incorporate lime juice and Angostura bitters around 1947. This iteration, called the Fig Leaf, looked a lot like the cocktail known today as the Crescent City. Since our recipe comes from an old Angostura promotional pamphlet, it's hard to say who deserves the credit for its creation. But it's easy to believe that this cocktail originated in the port city of New Orleans, with its abundant supplies of fortified wines and rum. Clearly, whoever created it had New Orleans in mind. It was nick-named Crescent City after the distinctive curved shape of the French Quarter, the oldest part of the city, built in the crook of a sharp bend in the Mississippi River.

1½ ounces Cocchi vermouth di Torino

½ ounce Hamilton Jamaican Pot Still Black Rum or other Jamaican rum

½ ounce freshly squeezed lime juice

¼ ounce Turbinado Syrup (page 192)

1 dash Angostura bitters

Pour the vermouth, rum, lime juice, syrup, and bitters into a cocktail shaker. Fill the shaker with ice cubes. Close and shake vigorously 20 times. Fine-strain into the chilled glass.

Mississippi Punch

Barware Rocks glass + straw   **Serving ice** Crushed

This cocktail, first printed in Jerry Thomas's *The Bar-Tender's Guide*, originated somewhere "along the Mississippi," according to cocktail historian David Wondrich. The drink was allegedly created as an ode to bare-knuckle boxing, popular in the South at the time. Boxing champion John L. Sullivan was known to say that the only fight he ever lost was to whiskey, prompting the creation of this boozy drink. The original formula calls for Jamaican rum, but we use rhum agricole to make this cocktail a bit more "punchy."

½ ounce Rhum JM agricole blanc

½ ounce cognac, such as Pierre Ferrand 1840

½ ounce 100-proof bonded rye whiskey

½ ounce freshly squeezed lemon juice

½ ounce Simple Syrup (page 193)

1 dash Angostura bitters

GARNISH

2 or 3 mint sprigs

1 fresh blackberry

1 lemon wheel

Powdered sugar

Fill the glass with crushed ice. Pour the rhum, cognac, rye, lemon juice, syrup, and bitters into a cocktail shaker. Fill the shaker with ice cubes. Cover and shake vigorously 20 times. Strain into the glass. Place the straw in the glass.

To garnish, press the mint sprigs between your fingers to release their aroma and tuck them into the ice next to the straw. Place the blackberry on the lemon wheel and secure it with a cocktail pick. Place the wheel on top of the crushed ice and dust them with the powdered sugar (see page 11).

Chatham Artillery Punch

Barware Punch bowl + rocks glasses   **Serving ice** 4 cups 1¼-inch cubes

Country and social clubs throughout the South have a grand tradition of creating house punches for their members to sip as they socialize. In Savannah, Georgia, the Chatham Artillery local volunteer militia, formed in 1786, came up with this seductive and potent punch.

Note that the lemon zest and sugar mixture, known as "oleo saccharum," must stand for at least 2 hours (or ideally overnight) to give the zest time to release as much of its aromatic oil as possible.

½ cup granulated sugar

Zest of 3 lemons

½ (750 ml) bottle 100-proof bonded bourbon

3 ounces cognac, such as Pierre Ferrand 1840

1 ounce Jamaican rum

3½ ounces freshly squeezed lemon juice

1 (750 ml) bottle blanc de blanc sparkling wine

Whole nutmeg

GARNISH

12 mint sprigs

12 blackberries

2 lemons, each sliced crosswise into 6 wheels

In a punch bowl, muddle the sugar and lemon zest until the sugar is saturated in lemon oil. Cover the bowl. Let stand at least 2 hours and preferably overnight (no more than 2 days).

Add the bourbon, cognac, rum, lemon juice, and sparkling wine to the punch bowl. Stir until the sugar is completely dissolved. Use tongs to remove and discard the lemon zests. Add the ice cubes and a few grates of nutmeg to the punch bowl and stir a few times. Ladle individual servings into 10 to 12 glasses.

To garnish each serving, press 1 mint sprig between your fingers to release its aroma. Fold a lemon wheel around the mint sprig and 1 blackberry and skewer with a cocktail pick. Lay the garnish on the rim of the glass.

Hurricane

Barware Hurricane glass + straw   **Serving ice** Crushed

The Hurricane was created by Louis Culligan at Pat O'Brien's Bar on St. Peter's Street in New Orleans. As the story goes, due to shortages of whiskey during World War II, liquor distributors pushed rum onto bar owners. To secure just one bottle of precious whiskey they had to purchase a case of rum, which inspired the bartenders at Pat O'Brien's to make Hurricanes by the dozen.

1 ounce Demerara rum, such as El Dorado 5-year

½ ounce Hamilton Jamaican Pot Still Black rum or other Jamaican rum

¾ ounce BG Reynolds passion fruit syrup

½ ounce freshly squeezed lemon juice

¼ ounce Turbinado Syrup (page 192)

GARNISH

2 or 3 mint sprigs

1 lemon wedge

Fill the glass with crushed ice. Pour the Demerara rum, Jamaican rum, passion fruit, lemon juice, and syrup into a cocktail shaker. Fill the shaker with ice cubes. Shake vigorously 20 times. Strain into the glass. Place the straw in the glass.

To garnish, press the mint sprigs between your fingers to release their aroma and tuck them into the ice next to the straw. Place the lemon wedge on the rim of the glass.

Vieux Carré

Barware 5.5-ounce cocktail coupe, chilled (see page 6)   **Serving ice** None

The historic French Quarter of New Orleans is often called the *Vieux Carré*, or "old square." The area's namesake cocktail (pronounced vu-ka-RAY) was created in 1938 at the Carousel Bar in The Monteleone, one of the city's oldest hotels, by the head bartender Walter Bergeron. It's a close relative of the Manhattan and the Sazerac. If you rinse the cocktail coupe with absinthe, you have a Cocktail de la Louisiane.

¾ ounce cognac, such as Pierre Ferrand 1840

¾ ounce 100-proof bonded rye whiskey

¾ ounce sweet vermouth, such as Cocchi di Torino

2 barspoons Bénédictine liqueur

2 dashes Angostura bitters

2 dashes Peychaud's bitters

GARNISH

1 lemon twist

Pour the cognac, rye, vermouth, Bénédictine, Angostura bitters, and Peychaud's bitters into a mixing glass. Fill the glass with ice cubes. Stir 20 times with a barspoon. Strain into the chilled glass. Garnish with the lemon twist.

Old-Fashioned

Barware Rocks glass   **Serving ice** 1 (2-inch) cube

The old-fashioned is in many ways the original cocktail—a concoction of spirit, bitters, sugar, and water. The word *cocktail* has become much broader since the introduction of fortified wines, exotic cordials, and bitters and elixirs into the original formula. This changed the word's meaning so much that people began to order the original cocktail "the old-fashioned way"—hence, the old-fashioned.

There are many claims as to where this drink was invented and by whom, but it's all hogwash: the old-fashioned is a precursor to almost all the drinks we know today. Many variations exist, and many include muddled fruit. This habit originated during Prohibition to hide the rough taste of the spirits of the day, and it persisted (sadly) even after better quality spirits reappeared. The contemporary old-fashioned has become synonymous with a whiskey cocktail, and at Julep we choose bourbon, not rye, to make it more sultry.

2 ounces 100-proof bonded bourbon

1 barspoon Turbinado Syrup (page 192)

2 dashes Angostura bitters

1 dash Abbott's bitters

GARNISH

1 swath orange zest

Place the ice cube in the glass. Pour the bourbon, syrup, Angostura bitters, and Abbott's bitters into a mixing glass. Fill the glass with ice cubes. Stir 20 times with a barspoon. Strain into the rocks glass.

Garnish with the orange zest.

Brandy French 75

Barware 8-ounce champagne flute   **Serving ice** None

When first published in *The Savoy Cocktail Book* in 1930, the formula for the French 75 called for gin. Later some asserted that the original cocktail had been made with cognac. Either way, the drink allegedly had such a kick that it was compared to a French 75mm field gun—hence the name. Over the past century, one city in particular has carried on the tradition of the French 75: New Orleans. This is logical because the drink exemplifies the city's French roots, which prevail to this day.

1½ ounces cognac, such as Pierre Ferrand 1840

¾ ounce freshly squeezed lemon juice

½ ounce Turbinado Syrup (page 192)

Sparkling wine, for topping off

GARNISH

1 lemon twist

Pour the cognac, lemon juice, and syrup into a cocktail shaker. Fill the shaker with ice cubes. Cover and shake vigorously 20 times. Fine-strain into the glass. Top off with sparkling wine.

Garnish with the lemon twist.

Pimm's Cup

Barware Collins glass   **Serving ice** 1¼-inch cubes

This modern Southern classic is rooted in nineteenth-century London, where James Pimm, owner of an oyster bar, created a liqueur to go with his shellfish. It eventually became a bottled product called Pimm's No. 1 Cup. On this side of the Atlantic, the Napoleon Hotel in New Orleans made the Pimm's Cup cocktail famous. For decades it has been their house drink, and it's still enormously popular. If you use dry ginger ale, as I do, adding the barspoon of Simple Syrup lends just enough sweetness to balance the drink.

1½ ounces Pimm's Cup

½ ounce London dry gin, such as Beefeater

½ ounce freshly squeezed lemon juice

1 barspoon Simple Syrup (page 193; optional)

Ginger ale, for topping off

GARNISH

1 cucumber strip (see Note)

Fill the glass with ice cubes. Add the Pimm's, gin, lemon juice, and syrup. Stir with a barspoon. Top off with the ginger ale.

To garnish, slide the cucumber strip down the inside of the glass so that most of it is submerged and the top 2 to 3 inches curl over the rim of the glass.

Note To make a cucumber strip, run a vegetable peeler down the length of a peeled cucumber.

Pendennis Club

Barware 7.5-ounce cocktail coupe, chilled (see page 6)   **Serving ice** None

The Pendennis Club in Louisville, Kentucky, a famous social club established in 1881, claims to be the birthplace of the old-fashioned cocktail. While this is disputable, what's certain is that they invented this cocktail and named it after the club. The original recipe called for gin (that would have been old-style or Old Tom gin, not London dry), lime, Peychaud's bitters, sugar, and apricot brandy. The Pendennis Club is in full swing to this day, known for its exclusive, lavish events for members—most notably the celebration of the annual Kentucky Derby.

1½ ounces Old Tom gin

¾ ounce Rothman & Winter apricot liqueur

½ ounce freshly squeezed lime juice

1 barspoon Turbinado Syrup (page 192)

1 barspoon Peychaud's bitters

GARNISH

1 lime wheel

Pour the gin, liqueur, lime juice, syrup, and bitters into a cocktail shaker. Fill the shaker with ice cubes. Cover and shake vigorously 20 times. Fine-strain into the chilled glass. Garnish with the lime wheel.

Ramos Gin Fizz

Barware Skinny collins glass   **Serving ice** None

This classic, gin-based cocktail has been written about so often that there's not much left to say. Henry C. Ramos created the drink in New Orleans in the 1880s, and it takes a hell of a long time to make. Bars used to employ a "Ramos line" to prepare the drink: a row of bartenders each took a turn shaking the drink before passing it down the line. Machines were even created to make the shaking process less laborious. But if, like us, you have neither a Ramos line nor a dedicated machine to mix the drink, five to eight minutes of shaking can seem like an eternity. So here are a few tips to keep in mind: Start out with dry hands, or they'll freeze to the shaker. Stand with a supported back. Find a comfortable range of motion. Keep your arms and shoulders loose. Allow your body to correct itself. Finally, remember that it's a marathon, not a sprint, so pace yourself. And if the drink hasn't reached the full volume of the glass the first time you pour it, you can always pour it back in and shake again—even several times. This cocktail does take a little time to master (it's difficult to whip meringue in a glass!), but ultimately it's worth every single shake.

2 ounces London dry gin, such as Beefeater

½ ounce freshly squeezed lime juice

½ ounce freshly squeezed lemon juice

¾ ounce Simple Syrup (page 193)

¾ ounce heavy cream

1 egg white

6 drops orange flower water

1 ounce soda water, for topping off

GARNISH

Whole nutmeg

Pour the gin, lime juice, lemon juice, syrup, cream, egg white, and orange flower water into a cocktail shaker. Cover and dry shake vigorously 20 times. Open and fill the shaker with ice cubes. Cover (make sure the shaker is tightly sealed) and shake 5 to 8 minutes until it sounds like a light horse gallop.

Strain into the glass. If there's not enough volume to reach the rim of the glass, pour it back into the cocktail shaker, add a few more ice cubes, shake it again, and strain it back into the glass. (Do this as many times as necessary). Let stand for a few seconds. Meanwhile, measure 1 ounce of soda water into a jigger and set aside.

Lightly tap the glass on the table until you see air bubbles popping on the surface of the drink and the glass feels like it's gently bouncing. Use a straw to make an indentation in the center of the mixture. Pour the soda water into the indentation. The cocktail will soufflé about ¼ inch above the rim.

Garnish with a few grates of nutmeg.

Old Pepper

Barware Rocks glass + straw **Serving ice** Crushed

This isn't technically a Southern classic, but it drinks so much like one that I couldn't imagine this chapter without it. The cocktail was actually created at a modern speakeasy in New York City called Milk & Honey, but every time I serve it at an event in the South, people absolutely love it.

1½ ounces 80-proof bourbon

¾ ounce Turbinado Syrup (page 192)

½ ounce freshly squeezed lemon juice

¼ ounce Crystal hot sauce

3 dashes Worcestershire sauce

GARNISH

1 chile de arbol

Fill the glass with crushed ice. Pour the bourbon, syrup, lemon juice, hot sauce, and Worcestershire sauce into a cocktail shaker. Fill the shaker with ice cubes. Cover and shake vigorously 20 times. Strain into the glass. Place the straw in the glass.

To garnish, place the chile on the ice.

Creole Contentment

Barware 7.5-ounce cocktail coupe, chilled (see page 6)   **Serving ice** None

It is said that this cocktail was created by an Episcopal bishop and discovered by Charles Baker in New Orleans, who published it in his 1939 book *The Gentleman's Companion*. We don't know much more about the story, but the *Creole* in the cocktail's title could refer to the French settlers and their cherished cognac. Moreover, New Orleans was a booming port town with many Portuguese settlers, so there was plenty of madeira available. It makes sense that someone would think of combining these two spirits and—if it was indeed an Episcopal bishop—that the resulting cocktail would be named Contentment. The original recipe called for equal parts cognac and madeira, but Baker is credited with altering it to the recipe that is popular today.

1½ ounces cognac, such as Pierre Ferrand 1840

1 ounce rainwater madeira

½ ounce Luxardo maraschino liqueur

2 dashes Regans' orange bitters

1 swath lemon zest

Pour the cognac, madeira, maraschino, and bitters into a mixing glass. Fill the glass with ice cubes. Stir 20 times with a barspoon. Strain into the chilled glass. Hold the lemon zest with the outer side of the peel directly over the cocktail and gently fold it over the drink to express the citrus oil into the cocktail.

Absinthe Suissesse

Barware Standard white wine glass   **Serving ice** None

For nearly two hundred years, the Old Absinthe House bar has been a staple of life in the Vieux Carré. Located on the corner of Rue Bourbon and Rue Bienville, the copper-topped wooden bar charms patrons as they sip their favorite beverages amid the sights and sounds of the French Quarter. And the Absinthe Suissesse is the staple drink at the Old Absinthe House. There are many variations of this cocktail, also known as a great morning-after remedy.

1½ ounces absinthe, preferably Kübler

½ ounce crème de menthe, preferably Tempus Fugit

½ ounce orgeat

2 barspoons Turbinado Syrup (page 192)

1 ounce heavy cream

1 egg white

GARNISH

Whole nutmeg

Pour the absinthe, crème de menthe, orgeat, syrup, cream, and egg white into a cocktail shaker. Dry shake vigorously 20 times. Fill the shaker with ice cubes. Close the shaker and shake vigorously 100 times. Fine-strain into the glass.

Garnish with a few grates of nutmeg.

Milk Punch

Barware Collins glass   **Serving ice** 3 (1¼-inch) cubes

This New Orleans holiday season classic was originally made with bourbon and served hot, either in a big punch bowl batch or as a single serving. When the hot milk was added to the bourbon, it would curdle and need to be strained before serving. Eventually the punch was made with heavy cream for a more lush result, and the higher fat content prevented curdling. At Julep, we follow the same basic recipe but always serve the punch cold, because in Houston the hot days far outnumber the cold ones.

1½ ounces 100-proof bonded bourbon

¾ ounce Turbinado Syrup (page 192)

3 ounces heavy cream

8 drops vanilla extract

GARNISH

Whole nutmeg

Place the ice cubes in the glass. Pour the bourbon, syrup, cream, and vanilla extract into a cocktail shaker. Fill the shaker with ice cubes. Cover and shake 40 times. Strain into the glass.

Garnish with a few grates of nutmeg.

Saratoga Brace Up

Barware 8-ounce champagne flute   **Serving ice** None

This New Orleans original was first published in an 1887 update of Jerry Thomas's *The Bar-Tender's Guide*. It's a riff on the Morning Glory Fizz, replacing the scotch and egg white with brandy and a whole egg and reducing the absinthe.

1½ ounces cognac, such as Pierre Ferrand 1840

1 barspoon absinthe

1 barspoon freshly squeezed lemon juice

½ ounce Turbinado Syrup (page 192)

1 whole egg

GARNISH

1 star anise

Pour the cognac, absinthe, lemon juice, syrup, and egg into a cocktail shaker. Dry shake vigorously 20 times. Fill the shaker with ice cubes. Close the shaker and shake vigorously 100 times. Fine-strain into the glass.

Garnish with the star anise.

Bar Snacks

170
MARINATED OLIVES

172
FRIED ANCHOVY–
STUFFED OLIVES

174
FRIED FIDEO

175
PIMIENTO CHEESE

176
DEVILED EGGS

178
PICKLED SHRIMP WITH
ESCABECHE VEGETABLES

180
CRAB-CURRY SALAD

182
LOBSTER AMBROSIA

185
SUMMER SALAD

186
BURRATA SALAD

188
LEMON ICEBOX PIES

One thing people notice about our snack menu is the wide array of seafood on offer. This is partly because briny shellfish and fish are particularly good partners for cocktails, but it's also a nod to a major development in the South's culinary history: widespread access to ice, which revolutionized what later generations of Southerners would drink and eat. The innovations of the nineteenth century meant suppliers could move ice beyond the port cities to inland towns, enabling perishable foods, particularly seafood, to be transported to cities and towns throughout the region. In addition to ice's role in popularizing cocktails in warm climates, it also transformed the tables of rural Southerners, introducing them to new flavors. Even today, long after electric refrigeration has made shipping perishables an entirely ordinary practice, we can appreciate the enticement of new-to-us foods and flavors. Offering good food to guests is an essential part of being a great host, whether you're welcoming people into your home or your bar.

When you're serving cocktails, a few nibbles provide balance. Good nibbles don't have to be complicated. We rely on fresh, in-season ingredients and prepare them in straightforward, delicious ways. I think the bar snacks at Julep are so popular because they are satisfying but not highly produced. Part of that is by design and part is by necessity—we have a minimalist kitchen at Julep, so we have to keep it simple. This simplicity has another advantage: Everything we serve is easily made in a home kitchen and almost all of it can be prepared in advance. That means you spend less time in the kitchen after your guests arrive and more time enjoying cocktails with them.

Marinated Olives

Makes 4 cups

These slightly spicy olives are especially good paired with citrusy, light cocktails, such as the Snake-bit Sprout (page 69).

1 quart mixed olives

2 cups extra-virgin olive oil

6 thyme sprigs

6 star anise

4 garlic cloves, very thinly sliced

2 bay leaves

4 (3-inch) sprigs rosemary

2 (3-inch) cinnamon sticks, broken in half

1 tablespoon coriander seeds, cracked in a mortar and pestle

1 teaspoon red pepper flakes

⅛ teaspoon ground allspice

Peeled zest of 1 orange

Place the olives in a bowl. Combine the oil, thyme, star anise, garlic, bay leaves, rosemary, cinnamon, coriander, pepper flakes, allspice, and orange zest in a saucepan. Bring to simmer over medium heat. Pour the marinade over the olives.

Cover and refrigerate for at least 3 days and up to 1 week.

When ready to serve, bring the olives to room temperature. Using a slotted spoon, transfer the olives to a small bowl and serve.

Deviled Eggs

Makes 24 (serves 6 to 8)

Since opening Julep, we've had deviled eggs in one form or another on the menu. We've filled them with smoked fish dip, topped them with sweet relish, and even served them deep-fried and garnished with caviar. It doesn't seem to matter how we make them, they always fly out of the kitchen. Here is the tried-and-true version we serve most often.

12 large eggs, straight from the refrigerator

¼ cup Garlic Aioli (page 173)

2 teaspoons Dijon mustard

½ teaspoon Tabasco sauce

¼ teaspoon kosher salt

Thinly sliced celery, for garnish

Chopped green onion, for garnish

Paprika, for garnish

Place the eggs in a saucepan large enough to hold them in a single layer. Cover with cold water by 1 inch. Bring to a boil over high heat. Meanwhile, fill a large bowl with ice water. As soon as the water begins to boil, remove the pan from the heat, cover, and set aside for 10 minutes.

Using a slotted spoon, transfer the eggs to the ice water. As soon as they are cool enough to handle, peel them one at a time and return the peeled eggs to the ice water. When all of the eggs are peeled, remove them from the water and pat dry.

Cut the eggs in half lengthwise and gently remove the yolks. Set the yolks aside and refrigerate the whites until needed.

Press the yolks through a mesh strainer into a bowl. Add the aioli, mustard, Tabasco, and salt and stir until well blended.

Use a small spoon or piping bag to fill each egg white with the filling. Cover and refrigerate for 1 hour or up to 2 days.

Just before serving, lay a few slices of celery on top of each deviled egg. Sprinkle with the green onion and paprika.

Crab-Curry Salad

Makes about 4 cups (serves 6 to 8)

A creamy crab salad served with club crackers and pickled okra fits beautifully with the Southern sensibility. But we think it has to have a little something extra to hold its own alongside a cocktail, so we kick it up with a spice mix that adds just the right zing.

1 pound jumbo lump crab

½ cup finely diced celery

¼ cup finely diced yellow onion

1 cup mayonnaise

2 tablespoons freshly squeezed lemon juice

2 tablespoons chopped flat-leaf parsley, plus whole leaves for garnish

2 tablespoons Jamaican Curry Seasoning, plus a pinch for garnish (recipe follows)

2 teaspoons kosher salt

1 teaspoon freshly ground black pepper

Celery leaves, for garnish

Turmeric, for garnish

Pickled okra, for serving

Ritz crackers, for serving

Place the crab in a mesh strainer. Gently break it apart with your fingers, removing any bits of shell. If the crab feels very moist, press lightly to remove excess liquid. Transfer the crab to a bowl.

Add the celery, onion, mayonnaise, lemon juice, 2 tablespoons of parsley, the curry seasoning, salt, and pepper. Stir gently until well combined.

Cover and refrigerate for at least 6 hours and up to 3 days.

When ready to serve, use a slotted spoon to transfer the salad to a serving bowl (so that any liquid that has collected is left behind). To garnish, sprinkle with the parsley and celery leaves and pinch of turmeric. Serve with the okra and crackers on the side.

JAMAICAN CURRY SEASONING

Makes about ¼ cup

This warm spice mix is also great rubbed on chicken or shrimp before grilling or broiling.

1½ teaspoons cumin seeds

1½ teaspoons yellow mustard seeds

1½ teaspoons anise seeds

1½ teaspoons coriander seeds

¾ teaspoon whole allspice

¾ teaspoon fenugreek seeds

1 tablespoon plus ¾ teaspoon turmeric

Place the cumin, mustard, anise, coriander, allspice, and fenugreek seeds in a small skillet. Toast over medium heat, stirring often, until aromatic, about 1 minute.

Transfer the seeds to a spice or coffee grinder and grind to a fine powder.

Transfer the mixture to a glass jar with a lid and stir in the turmeric.

Close the jar with the lid and store in an airtight container for up to 1 month.

Burrata Salad

Serves 4

Several complementary contrasts in texture, flavor, and color come together in this composed salad. The creamy, fresh burrata cheese contrasts with the crisp crostini; the peppery arugula counters the tangy savory jam; and the fresh, sweet cherry tomatoes meld everything together. Use your favorite store-bought or farmer's market–find tomato or onion jam.

½ cup good-quality tomato or onion jam

2 cups halved red cherry tomatoes or a combination of red and yellow cherry tomatoes

8 ounces burrata cheese

4 cups washed and dried arugula

16 small crostini or Melba toasts

Extra virgin olive oil, for drizzling

Maldon salt, for finishing

Spread 2 tablespoons of the jam on each of 4 salad plates. Divide the cherry tomatoes among the plates.

Carefully cut the burrata round(s) in half or in wedges and divide them among the plates. Scatter the arugula on each plate. Place 4 toasts on each salad.

Drizzle with olive oil, sprinkle with the Maldon salt, and serve.

Lemon Icebox Pies

Makes 8 pies

Lemon icebox pies are a beloved Southern tradition, and Maria cookies are a beloved Mexican one—so it seemed not only natural but absolutely necessary for them to come together here at Julep. Lots of cooks use Nilla Wafers blended with butter to make their icebox pie crust, but those often need to be baked or frozen so they stay together. With our galley kitchen set-up, we need our pies to be truly no-bake *and* no-freeze, making the vanilla-scented Maria cookies that I grew up with an ideal choice. They're not too sweet, and they hold up beautifully when layered with the creamy filling. Even better, they fit perfectly in my favorite jars for serving them—the 7.4-ounce "tulip" jars made by Weck (see Resources, page 205). The jars are stylish and sturdy—two qualities that matter in a busy bar (and a busy home). You don't need to buy a special jar for these pies, however, since they taste great no matter what they're served in. Any 7- to 8-ounce dish will work well.

FILLING

8 ounces cream cheese, softened

1 (8-ounce) can condensed milk

1 cup labne or sour cream

½ cup strained freshly squeezed lemon juice

1 teaspoon grated lemon zest

40 to 48 Goya Maria cookies

MERINGUE

4 large egg whites, at room temperature

1 cup granulated sugar

½ cup light corn syrup

½ teaspoon vanilla extract

¼ teaspoon cream of tartar

To make the filling, place cream cheese, condensed milk, labne or sour cream, and lemon juice and zest in a blender. Process until well blended. Set aside.

To assemble the pies, place one cookie in the bottom of each of eight 7.4-ounce Weck jars; the cookie should fit neatly inside the jars. Spoon about 1 tablespoon of the filling on top of each cookie and gently spread to completely cover the cookie. Top with another cookie. Continue layering in this way until all of the lemon cream has been used, topping with a cookie and using 5 to 6 cookies in each pie. Refrigerate the pies for at least 1 hour and up to 3 days.

To make the meringue, bring about 2 inches of water to a simmer in the bottom of a double boiler or a large saucepan. In the top of the double boiler or in a metal bowl that sits inside the pan without touching the water, place the egg whites, sugar, corn syrup, vanilla, and cream of tartar. Whisk over the heat until the sugar is dissolved and the foam is smooth and warm to the touch, about 5 minutes.

Remove the pan from the heat and beat with a hand-held electric mixer on low speed for about 10 seconds. Gradually increase the speed to high, beating at each level for about 10 seconds. Continue to beat on high speed until the meringue is cool to the touch, about 8 minutes. Use at once or store in a tightly covered container in the refrigerator for up to 1 day.

When ready to serve the pies, spoon a large dollop of meringue onto each top cookie. If desired, brown the meringue under the broiler for 1 to 3 minutes, watching closely, until golden brown. Serve at once.

House Staples

192
TURBINADO SYRUP

193
SIMPLE SYRUP

194
SWEET POTATO SYRUP

195
HONEY MIX

196
LIME CORDIAL

198
SALT TINCTURE

199
HOT CINNAMON TEA

200
SASSAFRAS TEA

201
SATSUMA JELLY

The recipes for syrups, infused liquors, garnishes, and other extras in this chapter and throughout the book are crucial to recreating many Julep cocktails in your home. They are the backbone of what we do, and almost all of them are unique to us. That exclusivity makes them essential, not only because without them it would be impossible to make many of our cocktails, but also because they allow us to explore our region through many different ingredients. Julep's staples are based on elements with rich Southern connotations. We make syrups from sweet potatoes, kumquats, peaches, and honey; a sun-dried lime cordial; our own pickled cocktail onions; and hot infused teas from sassafras and cinnamon. Thanks to these basics, I am able to tell so many textured stories of the South though my cocktails.

Turbinado Syrup

Makes about 2¼ cups (18 ounces)

In order to ensure that every batch of syrup turns out just like the one before, I always use Sugar in the Raw brand turbinado sugar. It's a very consistent product, and that's so important for a staple ingredient like this syrup.

2 cups Sugar in the Raw turbinado

1 cup water

Combine the turbinado sugar and water in a saucepan and stir to combine. Place over medium heat and bring to a gentle boil, stirring occasionally. Reduce the heat and simmer until the sugar is completely dissolved and the syrup is slightly thickened, about 3 minutes.

Remove from the heat and let cool. Transfer to a glass container with a tight-fitting lid and store in the refrigerator for up to 1 week.

Simple Syrup

Makes about 2¼ cups (18 ounces)

When we want a less molasses-y effect in a cocktail, we make the syrup with regular granulated sugar rather than turbinado.

2 cups granulated sugar

1 cup water

Combine the sugar and water in a small saucepan and stir to combine. Place over medium heat and bring to a gentle boil, stirring occasionally. Reduce the heat and simmer until the sugar is completely dissolved and the syrup is slightly thickened, about 3 minutes.

Remove from the heat and let cool. Transfer to a glass container with a tight-fitting lid and store in the refrigerator for up to 1 week.

Sweet Potato Syrup

Makes about 1 cup (8 ounces)

You'll need a juicer for this luscious syrup—the perfect excuse to buy one!

2 to 3 purple-skinned sweet potatoes, scrubbed and cut into pieces

¼ cup Sugar in the Raw turbinado

½ ounce cognac

Juice the sweet potatoes in a juicer; you should have 7 fluid ounces of juice.

Transfer the juice to a saucepan and stir in the sugar. Bring to a gentle simmer over low heat. Gently simmer, stirring frequently, until the sugar is dissolved, 20 to 25 minutes.

Remove from the heat and let cool completely. Stir in the cognac.

Store in a covered container in the refrigerator for up to 1 week. Shake before using.

Honey Mix

Makes about 1 cup (8 ounces)

Sometimes honey's particular flavor is just what a cocktail needs, but its thickness can prevent it from fully dissolving when added directly to the drink. Making the Honey Mix with water solves this problem.

Pour the honey into a glass measuring cup or a small bowl. Add the boiling water and stir until well combined. Use immediately or transfer to a covered container and store in the refrigerator for up to 1 week.

¾ cup honey   **¼ cup boiling water**

Lime Cordial

Makes about 1 cup (8 ounces)

A cordial is a sweet, concentrated drink. This particular cordial is fragrant and easy to make using dried limes (see Two Drinks Coming, page 77). It's delicious in gimlets as well.

1 cup granulated sugar

1 cup water

5 ounces dried limes

Combine the sugar, water, and limes in a small saucepan, breaking up the limes slightly as you add them to the pan. Stir to combine. Place over medium heat and bring to a gentle boil, stirring occasionally. Reduce the heat and simmer until the sugar is completely dissolved and the syrup is slightly thickened, about 5 minutes.

Remove from the heat and strain the hot cordial through a fine-mesh strainer or a mesh strainer lined with cheesecloth into a clean container.

Use immediately or transfer to a glass jar with a tight-fitting lid. Store in the refrigerator for up to 1 month.

Salt Tincture

Makes about ½ cup (4 ounces)

This tincture is used in the Preservationist (page 96) to add a good dose of salinity. It may seem as if this recipe yields a lot, but you'll be amazed at how many different ways you can use it. Salt tincture is especially useful to have on hand to balance the citrus in cocktails. For instance I add it to margaritas when the limes are too tart, which often happens when they've been grown in warmer weather.

Combine the salt and neutral grain spirit in a glass jar with a lid. Tightly close the jar and let stand at room temperature for 2 weeks, shaking the jar about once a day. Before using the tincture, transfer it to a bitters bottle. In a closed container, the tincture will keep at room temperature for up to 6 months.

½ cup sea salt flakes, such as Maldon

½ cup overproof neutral grain spirit, such as Everclear

Hot Cinnamon Tea

Makes about 1½ cups (12 ounces)

It's not enough to simply put cinnamon sticks directly into boiling water. In order to fully release their flavor, you need to first boil them in the water for a couple of minutes.

2 cups water

2 (3-inch) cinnamon sticks

Bring the water and cinnamon sticks to a boil in a small saucepan. Boil for 2 minutes. Reduce the heat and simmer until the tea is a deep amber color, 8 to 10 minutes. Remove the cinnamon sticks (reserve them to use as a garnish).

Use immediately or cool completely and store in a covered container in the refrigerator for up to one week. Reheat before using.

Sassafras Tea

Makes about 1½ cups (12 ounces)

Make sure to use food-safe sassafras root bark, which can be found online.

2 cups water

Generous ½ cup food-grade sassafras root bark

Bring the water and sassafras root to a boil in a small saucepan. Boil gently, uncovered, for 10 minutes. Let cool to room temperature. Strain the tea; discard the sassafras root.

Use immediately or store in a covered container in the refrigerator for up to 1 week.

Satsuma Jelly

Makes six (8-ounce) jars

This nice, firm jelly imparts a bright orange flavor and very pretty color to the Rail to Satsuma (page 50). Satsumas are sweet and juicy, worth seeking out when they're in season during the late fall. But you can certainly use regular oranges or tangerines. This recipe necessarily makes a lot (it's hard to make a small amount of jelly), but since it's processed in canning jars, it can be stored in your pantry for at least a few months. It's delicious on toast.

4 cups freshly squeezed Satsuma, tangerine, or orange juice

2 teaspoons freshly squeezed lemon juice

1 (1.75-ounce) package Sure-Jell

5 cups sugar

Place six clean 8-ounce (½-pint) canning jars right-side up on a rack in a boiling water canner. Fill the canner with water to cover the jars by 1 inch. Bring the water to a simmer. Keep the jars in the hot water until ready to fill.

Meanwhile, wash the canning lids and rings in warm, soapy water and rinse thoroughly. Set aside to dry.

Combine the Satsuma or orange juice, lemon juice, and Sure-Jell in a saucepan. Bring to a boil, stirring constantly. When the mixture reaches a boil that won't die down even while stirring, cook 1 minute longer.

Stir in the sugar and return the mixture to a vigorous boil. Boil, stirring constantly, for 1 minute. Remove the pan from heat.

Use a jar lifter to remove the jars from the canner, carefully pouring the water inside each jar back into the canner. Pour the jelly into the jars, filling each jar to ¼ inch from the top rim (a jar funnel makes it easy to do this without spilling the hot mixture).

Carefully wipe the rims and sides of each jar. Place the lids on top and screw the rings on, tightening them by hand.

Place the filled jars on the rack in the water canner. Make sure the water in the canner covers the jars by 1 to 2 inches, adding more as needed.

Cover the canner and bring the water to a rolling boil. Boil for 10 minutes. Turn off the heat and uncover. Let stand for 5 minutes.

Use a jar lifter to carefully remove the jars and place them on a towel on the counter. Let the jars stand without moving them for 24 hours.

Check the jars to make sure they are properly sealed: Press on the center of each jar; it should not flex. Unscrew each ring and try to lift the lids with your fingers. If they can't be lifted, the seal is good. Screw the rings back on, label the jars, and store in a dark, cool place for up to 1 year. (If the center of a jar flexes when pressed or the lid can be removed, refrigerate that jar and use within 1 week.)

Cocktail Onions

Makes about 3 cups

It's certainly easy to find store-bought cocktail onions in most liquor stores, but when they're a garnish in a boozy cocktail, we really want them to shine. That's why we much prefer to pickle our own, which we have just the right brine.

1 tablespoon juniper berries

2 teaspoons yellow mustard seeds

3 to 4 cups small pearl onions, peeled or as needed (see Note)

2 cups Champagne vinegar

½ cup Banyuls wine vinegar

1 tablespoon sea salt

1 tablespoon granulated sugar

Have ready a clean 1-quart canning jar, canning lid, and ring.

Place the jar right side up on a rack in a boiling water canner or other tall pot. Fill the canner with water to cover the jar by 1 inch. Bring the water to a simmer. Keep the jar in the hot water until ready to fill.

Meanwhile, wash the canning lid and ring in warm, soapy water and rinse thoroughly. Set aside to dry.

Use a jar lifter to remove the jar from the canner, carefully pouring the water inside the jar back into the canner. Place the juniper berries and mustard seeds in the jar. Fill the jar to the top with the onions. Set aside.

Combine the Champagne vinegar, Banyuls vinegar, salt, and sugar in a saucepan. Bring to a boil, stirring constantly until the salt and sugar are dissolved. Pour the hot mixture into the jar, filling to ½ inch from the top rim. Carefully wipe the rims and sides of the jar. Place the lid on top and screw the ring on, tightening it by hand.

Place the filled jar on the rack in the water canner. Make sure the water in the canner covers the jar by 1 to 2 inches, adding more water as needed. Cover the canner and bring the water to a rolling boil. Boil for 3 minutes. Turn off the heat and uncover the canner. Let stand for 5 minutes.

Use a jar lifter to carefully remove the jar and place on a towel on the counter. Let the jar stand without moving them for 24 hours.

Check the jar to make sure it is properly sealed: Press on the center; it should not flex. Unscrew the ring and try to lift the lid with your fingers. If it can't be lifted, the seal is good. Screw the ring back on, label the jar, and store in a dark, cool place for 3 days before using. Store for up to 1 year. (If the center of the jar flexes when pressed or the lid can be removed, refrigerate jar and use within 1 week.)

Note Peel the outer 1 or 2 layers of any very large pearl onions so that they are all the same size. Keep the ends of the onions intact so they don't fall apart.

Resources

Ingredients and Tools

AIRLINE SEAFOOD

Texas Shell Shock Boil Blend
713–526–2351

ANSON MILLS

Benne seeds and Carolina rice
ansonmills.com

COCKTAIL KINGDOM

Bar tools
cocktailkingdom.com

UMAMI MART

Bar tools
umamimart.com

WEBRESTAURANT STORE

Soda siphons and CO_2 cartridges
webrestaurantstore.com

WECK JARS

Canning jars
weckjars.com

Other Resources

DAVID WONDRICH'S BOOKS ABOUT THE HISTORY OF COCKTAILS

Imbibe! Updated and Revised Edition: From Absinthe Cocktail to Whiskey Smash, a Salute in Stories and Drinks to "Professor" Jerry Thomas, Pioneer of the American Bar (TarcherPerigee, 2015)

Punch: The Delights (and Dangers) of the Flowing Bowl (TarcherPerigee, 2010)

SOUTHERN FOODWAYS ALLIANCE

southernfoodways.org
This organization explores the food cultures of the American South. I especially love *Gravy*, the quarterly magazine and weekly podcast that they produce (southernfoodways.org/gravy).

FOR INFORMATION ABOUT THE CIVIL WAR

Trading with the Enemy: The Covert Economy During the American Civil War, by Philip Leigh (Westholme, 2014)

About the Authors

orn in Mexico and raised in Texas, **Alba Huerta** is a proud Mexican-American Houstonian. After her very first job, which was working in a bar, it wasn't long before she was bartending and building expertise as a service professional. Next, she moved to hospitality-focused Las Vegas to refine her service skills, speed, efficiency, and the ability to coordinate and execute a volume of large projects. After a few years, Alba returned to Houston and, in 2011, was recruited to be the general manager of Anvil Bar and Refuge, during which time she helped launch the Houston chapter of the United States Bartenders' Guild and became involved in the Tequila Interchange Project. Before opening Julep, Alba partnered on another Houston bar, The Pastry War, a Mezcaleria that reflects her high-quality standards for agave production. In 2014 she opened Julep to a very warm reception. Julep was one of four finalists for Best New American Cocktail Bar at Tales of the Cocktail's 2015 Spirited Awards and has been featured in many national publications since, from *Garden & Gun* to the *New York Times Magazine*. Julep was named one of the top five bars in the United States by *Bon Appétit* in 2015 and one of the twenty-four best bars in America by *Esquire* in 2017.

Alba was named Bartender of the Year in 2014 by *Imbibe* magazine and one of Houston's 50 Most Fascinating People by the *Houston Chronicle*. She has been featured on the cover of *Texas Monthly* and *Southwest Magazine*. In 2015, *Food & Wine* selected her as one of ten rising-star female mixologists and Thrillist chose her as one of the Best Bartenders in America. She was the featured mixologist at the Southern Foodways Alliance's 2013 Symposium and again in 2015, after which she was elected to serve as a board member. She was inducted into Tales of the Cocktail's Dames Hall of Fame in 2012.

Above all, Alba is known for bringing her passion for quality wine, spirits, and cocktails and her warmth and Southern hospitality to her bars and her profession.

***

Marah Stets is a *New York Times*–bestselling writer and editor. She lives in the Washington, D.C., area with her family.

Index

Copyright © 2018 by Alba Huerta
Photographs copyright © 2018 by Julie Soefer

All rights reserved.
Published in the United States by Lorena Jones Books, an imprint of Crown Publishing Group,
a division of Penguin Random House LLC, New York.
www.crownpublishing.com
www.tenspeed.com

Lorena Jones Books and the Lorena Jones Books colophon are trademarks of Penguin
Random House, LLC.

Library of Congress Cataloging-in-Publication Data is on file with the publisher

Hardcover ISBN: 978-0-399-57941-7
eBook ISBN: 978-0-399-57942-4

Printed in China

Satsuma Jelly recipe on page 201 reprinted with the permission of Brennan's of Houston

Design by Betsy Stromberg
Photo styling by Amanda Medsger
Glassware courtesy of Kuhl-Linscomb, Houston, Texas

10 9 8 7 6 5 4 3 2 1

First Edition